HOW TO DO FINANCIAL ASSET INVESTIGATIONS

ABOUT THE AUTHOR

Ronald Mendell is a graduate of Regents College in Albany, New York. A frequent contributor to *Security Management* magazine, he currently is a freelance writer on security and investigative topics in Austin, Texas. He wrote *Investigating Computer Crime: A Primer for Security Managers* in 1998 that is also published by Charles C Thomas, Publisher, Ltd.

Second Edition

HOW TO DO FINANCIAL ASSET INVESTIGATIONS

A Practical Guide for Private
Investigators, Collections Personnel,
and Asset Recovery Specialists

By

RONALD L. MENDELL, B.S., C.L.I.

Certified Legal Investigator
Member, American Society for Industrial Security (ASIS)
Austin, Texas

Charles C Thomas
PUBLISHER • LTD.
SPRINGFIELD • ILLINOIS • U.S.A.

Published and Distributed Throughout the World by

CHARLES C THOMAS • PUBLISHER, LTD.
2600 South First Street
Springfield, Illinois 62794-9265

ISBN 0-398-07044-X (cloth)
ISBN 0-398-07045-8 (paper)

Library of Congress Catalog Card Number: 99-054997

First Edition, 1994
Second Edition, 2000

With THOMAS BOOKS *careful attention is given to all details of manufacturing
and design. It is the Publisher's desire to present books that are satisfactory as to their
physical qualities and artistic possibilities and appropriate for their particular use.*
THOMAS BOOKS *will be true to those laws of quality that assure a good name
and good will.*

Printed in the United States of America
SM-R-3

Library of Congress Cataloging-in-Publication Data

Mendell, Ronald L.
    How to do financial asset investigations : a practical guide for private
investigators, collections personnel, and asset recovery specialists / by
Ronald L. Mendell.--2nd ed.
        p.   cm.
    Includes bibliographical references and index.
    ISBN 0-398-07044-X (cloth) -- ISBN 0-398-07045-8 (paper)
    1. Collecting of accounts--United States--Handbooks, manuals, etc.   2.
Private investigators--United States. 3. Records--United States. 4. Assets
(Accounting). I. Title.
HG3752.7.U6 M46 2000
363.2'52--dc21

                                                                            99-054997

To Judy, Buddy, and Duchess.

PREFACE TO THE FIRST EDITION

Often, when trying to collect on a judgment or a debt, the investigator or collections professional confronts a stone wall. The debtor claims to lack the necessary funds to satisfy the debt. This book serves as a practical primer in overcoming this obstacle. Emphasizing the use of data collection forms and the latest computer technology, the text offers tools for identifying, locating, and assessing debtors' assets and liabilities.

While traditional texts usually discuss only print sources, this book explains data gathering from computer databases, CD-ROM, human sources, surveillance, and public records. The topics cover both individuals and businesses. They range from obtaining subjects' basic identifiers, such as a social security number, to using key business ratios to calculate figures for a company's balance sheet. The text explains how to integrate the data into a total picture.

The proper techniques for correlating data receive due emphasis. A financial investigator works with information from dissimilar sources. A non-financial document such as a courthouse criminal file may lead to a great deal of financial information about a person. Learning how to exploit these informational trails is the book's key subject area.

Judging the validity of the debtor's claimed liabilities and assets is an often missed part of the investigative equation. Subjects of an investigation may try to cloud the issues by introducing bogus assets or liabilities. Cutting through these smoke screens is a main theme of the book. Additionally, the art of finding hidden assets receives the space of an entire chapter; something not found in most financial investigative works.

The reader will find in the text ample forms for gathering, organizing, and analyzing data. There are special forms for individuals and businesses. Form design allows for easy integration of information.

R.L.M.

PREFACE TO THE SECOND EDITION

Financial asset investigation continues to evolve through its techniques. And, while the fundamental principles outlined in the 1994 edition remain sound, this revision strives to incorporate more online and electronic sources. The Internet marches on as an essential tool for investigators, and financial sleuths need to take every advantage of its treasures.

And, the new edition reflects the Internet's influence by adding a new Chapter 13, "Investigating Using the Internet and Other Sources." Taking the investigator through a fictional asset search in conjunction with a divorce, the chapter covers the Internet as a resource for obtaining facts on collectibles, stocks, bonds, insurance companies, foreign companies, and much more.

New sections added to existing chapters include "Financial Investigation: A Tool for Security Managers," "Piercing the Corporate Veil," "Newsgroups," and "Public Record Searching Shortcuts."

Since the security issues involving key employees often arise from financial problems, the new security section will relate the book's principles to needs of security managers doing background investigations.

Identifying businesses that masquerade as corporations has become an important skill in the asset investigation business. The new section provides an ample checklist needed to prove a corporation is really the alter ego of an individual or a group.

Newsgroups are the bulletin boards (or gossip boards) of the Internet They contain huge amounts of information on subjects ranging from collectibles to the details of incorporating in Zaire. Investigators need to understand how to access this source. This new section and Chapter 13 explore this little known resource.

Public record shortcuts, discussed in a new section, reveal three electronic sources that can save considerable time and trouble when looking for suits, liens, judgments, UCCs, and incorporation records. These new additions hopefully will make your hunting easier and more productive in the realm of financial asset investigation.

R.L.M.

CONTENTS

Preface to the First Edition   vii
Preface to the Second Edition   ix
Introduction   3
     Computers   4
     Summary   7
Chapter
     1.   OBTAINING THE IDENTIFIERS   8
     The Importance of Basic Identifiers   8
       The Social Security Number   9
       A Person's Name   9
       Address Histories   10
     Common Sources   10
       Trashing About   11
       Voters' Registration   11
       Record Searching Techniques   11
     Tools for Organizing Information   12
       The Telephone Book   13
     Courthouse Files   14
       Civil Court Records   14
     Other Common Sources   15
     Lesser Known Sources   15
     Financial Statements   16
     Professional Directories   17
     Governmental Records   18
     Summary   18
     2.   IDENTIFYING RELATIVES AND ASSOCIATES   20
     Basic Sources   20
       Motor Vehicle Address Searches   21
       The Local Newspaper on CD-ROM   21
       Other Miscellaneous Sources   22
     Other States and Localities   22
     Mailing Lists   24
     Securities and Exchange Commission   24

	Social Security Number	24
	Human Sources	26
	Summary	27
3.	BASIC SOURCES FOR INDIVIDUALS	30
	The Law Speaks	31
	Bankruptcy Records	33
	Occupational Information	35
	Vehicles	36
	Boats	36
	Aircraft	37
	UCC Filings	38
	Tax Liens	39
	Corporations: Officer/Director	40
	Real Estate Records	40
	Public Record Searching Shortcuts	42
	Summary	43
4.	INFORMATION BROKERS AND OTHER SOURCES	47
	Information Brokers	47
	Fair Credit Reporting Act (FCRA)	50
	Other Database Providers	50
	Business Sources	53
	Newsgroups	56
	Biographical Sources	57
	Research Centers	57
5.	VISITING THE SUBJECT'S PREMISES	59
	Drive-By of Residence	59
	Surveillance	61
	A Word About Trash	61
	Reading the Trash	62
	Neighbors	63
	Summary	63
6.	ADVANCED SOURCES FOR INDIVIDUALS	69
	How the Basic Search Differs	69
	Special Issues in Accident Cases	70
	Wage Earnings Information	70
	Governmental Sources	71
	Real Estate Records (A Second Look)	73
	Financial Statements	73
	Unreported Income	74

	Lawsuits (Another Look)	76
	Financial Investigations: A Tool for Security Managers	76
	Summary	78
7.	FINDING HIDDEN ASSETS	79
	Using Discovery Techniques	79
	Common Hiding Places	80
	The Paydown	81
	Life Insurance	81
	Money Orders and Other Negotiable Instruments	82
	Limited Partnerships	83
	Dead and Dissolved Corporations	84
	Stockbrokers	85
	Collectibles and Safe Deposit Boxes	85
	Overseas or Offshore Accounts and Businesses	86
	Other Financial Dodges	89
	Sweetheart Lawsuits	90
	Summary	91
8.	BASIC BUSINESS ASSET SEARCH	95
	Additional Financial Parameters	96
	Balance Sheets	96
	Scanning for Information	97
	CD-ROMs	99
	Other Basic Business Reference Sources	100
	State Filing Requirements	100
	Unincorporated Businesses	102
	Charitable and Non-Profit Organizations	103
	Business Credit Reports	103
	SEC Reports	104
	Other Information Sources (From Chapter Three)	105
	Personal Property Renderings	105
	Piercing the Corporate Veil	106
	Summary	108
9.	THE PLANT VISIT	113
	The Overview	113
	Site Security	115
	Going Inside	115
	Parking Lots, Storage Areas, and Delivery Areas	116
	Waste Disposal and Other Vendors	117
	Area Businesses	117

Additional Details   118
Summary   120
10. ADVANCED SOURCES FOR BUSINESSES   125
Identifying Those Who Can Tell More   125
Interviewing Techniques   127
Using Key Business Ratios   129
Business Intelligence Techniques   130
    What Constitutes Reliable Data?   130
    What Constitutes Valid Data?   131
Background on a Business   132
Summary   134
11. RECORDING DATA AND REPORTING
    TO THE CLIENT   138
Organizing Data   139
    Reorganizing and Analyzing Data   142
    The Association Summary   143
    The Banking Summary   143
Reporting on the Individual   145
The Business Report   147
Summary   148
12. A FICTIONAL PRELIMINARY INVESTIGATION   151
San Francisco   152
Cross-Texas Transport   153
The Main Players   153
Organizing the Data   154
The Key Piece: A Personal Bond   154
Blue Diamond vs Blue Star?   155
Intrepid Holdings   155
Melissa Reports   156
Interlocking Companies   156
Additional Newspaper Research   157
Business Credit Sources   158
Athena United Software   159
    Shivers' Hidden Interest   160
Jupiter's Credit Report   160
Banking Information   161
Legal Resource Index   161
Business Ratios   162
Biographical Background   163

Summary	163
13. INVESTIGATING USING THE INTERNET AND OTHER SOURCES	165
General Instructions for Mary	166
Corporations and Businesses	168
Stocks, Bonds, and Mutual Funds	170
Insurance	171
Financial Statements	172
Credit Cards	174
Income Tax Returns	174
Bank Statements and Checks	175
Real Estate	176
Vehicles, Boats, Aircraft	176
Calendars	177
Leases	177
Collectibles	178
Summary of Internet Resources	178
Bibliography	181
Index	185

HOW TO DO FINANCIAL
ASSET INVESTIGATIONS

INTRODUCTION

This book explores the practical techniques for financial asset investigation. Its readership should include legal and private investigators, collections specialists, and asset recovery professionals. The techniques presented will cover both individuals and businesses. While the text does mention some financial fraud schemes, the book is not a manual on white-collar crime, nor is it a handbook on investigating embezzlements. Rather, consider it a primer on how to find assets to satisfy judgments and debts.

Emphasizing the importance of public records, it will concentrate on research techniques. These methods make considerable use of libraries, periodicals, and governmental documents. Each chapter begins with a brief introduction stating its objectives and ends with a summary. Starting with investigations of individuals, the text progresses to discussing corporate and business inquiries. The constant theme will remain the need to correlate data from different sources. To move forward one must look not only ahead but to the right and left too.

Correlating data means that investigators must keep an open mind. Recognizing the use of non-financial records as tools is essential. The traffic accident report, the county court criminal file, or a newspaper account may all contain clues as to "who owns what." Integrate them into the search for background on your subject or target. In a nutshell, the book teaches that the more you taste of a target's life, the more you will learn about where the money comes and goes.

Another important theme is the investigator's need to understand local laws concerning privacy issues. An investigator must employ lawful methods when conducting financial investigations. Obtaining an individual's credit information carries legal pitfalls. Entering the subject's premises to gather information must not be intrusive. At the federal level, one should become familiar with the Fair Credit Reporting Act (FCRA). When discussing the subject of information brokers later in Chapter 4, we will explain how they can be a resource on the FCRA and your state's credit and privacy laws. Illegal methods such as wiretapping, the improper obtaining of credit files, and the improper use of informants are not the subject matter of this book.

In the course of your reading, this book will teach you:

1. How to Obtain Initial Identifiers on Individuals.
2. Identifying Relatives, Associates, and Friends of a Subject.
3. Researching Basic Sources on an Individual.
4. How to Use Information Brokers.
5. Effective Reconnaissance of the Subject's Premises.
6. Using Advanced Sources on an Individual.
7. Locating Hidden Assets.
8. Researching Basic Sources on a Business.
9. Doing an Effective Plant Visit.
10. Using Advanced Sources on a Business.
11. Recording Data and Reporting to the Client.

Concluding with fictional case studies, Chapter 12 demonstrates how the weaving together of diverse sources produces effective financial information; Chapter 13 demonstrates using the Internet as an investigative resource.

The book also has an ample bibliography for further reading. The author's hope is that the self-learning method introduced here will carry on into further reading and exploration. Financial investigation is a fascinating subject which continually yields new information for the investigator's tool kit. Attending seminars and networking among other investigators will keep your knowledge base current. Also, trading ideas is one of the great pleasures the investigative community offers.

COMPUTERS

Finally, this book stresses getting information from computers whenever possible. This does not mean that I feel computer-based data is somehow sacred or infallible. On the contrary, an investigator should treat computer-based information just like any other source: *subject to further confirmation*. Not seeking additional validation of what a computer database tells you is simple foolhardiness. However, modern investigators do themselves a great disservice in not utilizing computers as an investigative tool. Consider computers as an extension of your mental and sensory powers.

Scanning for information is so much faster by computer. One can run several names in the time it takes to check one name by manual methods. Some databases offer search capabilities that are virtually impossible by using printed sources. For example, one can request from the NEXIS/LEXIS periodical database all references to a fast-food company's franchise operations in Denver, Colorado from 1990. If you know that the company's regional franchise manager is John Jones, you can further limit the search to articles containing John's name.

Computers afford tremendous investigative power, if used wisely. They can be knowledge multipliers. Starting with a single piece of data, one can develop many investigative leads. The subject's name in a newspaper article on a CD-ROM disc leads to the name and location of his business, a description of the business, and the names of his relatives.

If you do not wish to begin learning about computers by buying your own machine, go to your local county clerk's office, public library, or university library. You will probably find that the computer indexes there do more than replace the old index book or card catalog. They serve as research tools. Do not be afraid to "play" with them. Search a name on several different databases, even if you feel a "hit" is unlikely. I think you will find many surprises. Adopt a creative attitude. Such surprises are the stuff of investigation: the aces up the sleeve, the hidden tricks.

In the next chapter, I will continue to use the term "database." I will also re-introduce the word "CD-ROM." To avoid any misunderstanding, let me define their meanings. A database is simply an organized collection of data available on a computer. The batting averages of all players in the American League would be a database. The names of each player, their team's name, and their individual batting average would each be a separate "field" on the database. A field is simply a convenient compartment to store similar data. In searching a database, I can do it by just one field: "Give me George Brett's average." Or, if the software allows, I can combine fields: "Give me the names of all players with the Yankees that have a batting average of .209."

The databases found in financial investigative work yield background, credit, and personal identifying information. Newspaper and periodical indexes like NEXIS/LEXIS, Legal Resource Index, or Business Periodical Index provide good historical or biographical material on subjects. National credit services like Chilton or Experian offer access to individual and business credit files. One can glean personal identifiers from governmental databases such as driving records, courthouse indexes, and state licensing agencies.

Databases come in several forms. They can be in a distant computer that an investigator accesses by a modem from their personal computer (PC). These are known as online services. DIALOG, NEXIS/LEXIS, America Online, and CompuServe are examples. Information brokers or resellers offer databases authored by a third party such as the Texas Secretary of State's Uniform Commercial Code (UCC) filings. Access to information brokers is through a modem. Like with the online services, in some cases the investigator directly communicates with the desired database after selecting it from a menu. Many times though, the requestor leaves an electronic message with the information broker. The information broker's staff researches the database and leaves the result in the requestor's electronic mailbox for later retrieval by modem.

Other databases require in-house use. Some libraries, governmental agencies, and private organizations do not permit off-site access. One has to use a terminal on the premises. Some will allow voice inquiries by telephone with a terminal operator doing the actual search. Investigators need to learn the resources available in their area.

Some databases are available on CD-ROM for use on PCs. CD-ROM stands for "Compact Disc-Read Only Memory." Just like musical compact discs, CD-ROMs cannot be recorded on or written to by the user. They contain huge amounts of data encoded digitally on their surface. One CD-ROM can hold the equivalent of 250,000 pages of text. To read one, the user must place the disc in a CD-ROM drive connected either externally or internally to a PC. Investigators will find CD-ROMs for large databases like National Newspaper Index, Business Periodical Index, MEDLINE (National Library of Medicine), and even their local newspaper, in public and university libraries. CD-ROM discs covering encyclopedias, business address databases, and the federal government's information resources are available for privately owned PCs. A close cousin to the CD-ROM, the DVD, can store vast amounts of information and images. Expect to see more of these technologies in the investigative world. They place enormous information at the disposal of the individual investigator.

SUMMARY

In this brief introduction, we encountered the book's major themes: (1) Cross-checking and correlating data builds a financial investigation. Paying close attention to sources that speak of an individual's background, life-style, and associates is a wise practice. (2) Conducting financial investigations within the law is not difficult. However, the investigator must learn the privacy and credit laws of the relevant jurisdiction. (3) Computer-based sources allow for effective scanning of databases for background and financial information on individuals and businesses. (4) Be on the lookout for knowledge multipliers: the article in a newspaper, the state license application, or the personal bond form. These types of data-intensive sources open many other informational avenues. (5) Many of the techniques applicable to individuals will work for businesses. Some investigations require developing case files on both the people and the associated companies. The text aims to make this a smooth, integrated process.

Chapter 1

OBTAINING THE IDENTIFIERS

Any financial inquiry must acquire certain basic data about a sub-ject before rigorous research begins. Not knowing a subject's date of birth or social security number may prevent you from positive iden-tification while examining public records. The lack of a full name, and any aliases used, may bar discovering key documents. If the last name is a common one, not possessing the middle name could render index-es unusable. Ignorance of the subject's address history may leave assets in other jurisdictions undiscovered.

Upon completing this chapter, you should know:

1. How to use effectively Basic Identifiers such as Date of Birth, Social Security Number, Names or Aliases, and Address History.
2. Common Sources for such Data: Voters' Registration, Tele-phone Directory, Courthouse Criminal Files, Driver's License Records, City Crisscross, Directory, Civil Records, or Trash.
3. Lesser Known Sources: Newspaper and Periodical Databases, Local Police Database, Municipal Court Database, Biographi-cal Reference Works, Special Historical Collections, Bankrupt-cy Court, State Regulatory and Licensing Agencies, and Financial Statements.

THE IMPORTANCE OF BASIC IDENTIFIERS

Many records use the date of birth (DOB) as a definitive identifi-er. One can access driving records in most states with a correct name and a DOB. Criminal files at both the courthouse and at the police station use the DOB as an essential part of a suspect's pedigree. The retrieval of medical records often requires this identifier. The same is true for academic records. Professional licenses granted by state or local agencies use DOB as a database field. Possessing a DOB for a subject makes searching these databases faster and easier. Effective researching of civil lawsuit records may require this key piece of data. Obviously, vital records such as birth certificates require knowledge of the DOB to obtain a copy. This little identifier provides great mileage in clarifying whether a person found in a record is the one you seek. It is a coveted tool for good investigators.

The Social Security Number

The social security number (SSN) has several applications. Most individual credit files use it as the key identifier. Therefore, doing nationwide credit searches requires knowing it. Many information brokers offer people-locating databases that require the number. Several states use the SSN as the driver's license number. The SSN also allows an investigator to discover the possible home state for a subject. The first three digits of the number reveal the state where social security account originated (see Chap. 2).

Banks and financial institutions use the SSN to allow access to account information and to identify customers. State regulatory and licensing agencies use the number as a searchable database field on professional licenses. State tax collection agencies and the Internal Revenue Service use the SSN to identify taxpayers.

Universities and other schools use the number as an identifier on academic records. Employers' payroll files have the number as a searchable field and as an employee identifier. To obtain military or veteran's records, one will need the subject's SSN. Other federal entitlement programs such as Medicaid, Medicare, and its namesake, Social Security, all use the SSN as a prime identifier. This number opens a multitude of financial, governmental, and employment records on a subject. Treat it as a precious passkey.

A Person's Name

The ultimate identifier is a person's correct, full name; without it the research of most records will be difficult or even futile. Obtaining the correct form of the name is the crux of the problem. Is it John Richardson Jones or John Richardsen Jones? Could it be Steve Hamilton Smith or Stephen Hamilton Smith? Was it the father Reginald K. Peterson or the son Reginald K. Peterson Jr.? Which is it, Amanda Dawn Jackson or Amanda Donna Jackson? Be sloppy with names and you will find yourself going down many dead-end trails.

A good investigator must also keep an eye and ear out for the use of aliases. Married women may have accounts and records in their maiden names. Individuals with "legal difficulties" will pick up and drop names like ordinary people change clothes. Divorces, remarriages, and changes in child custody will create new legal names. The proud owners of hyphenated surnames will not always employ them consistently. Persons responsible for recording customers' or clients" names will not be without error. The terminal operator may type in Peterson instead of Petersen, Johnson instead of Johnston. As our world becomes more computer-based, these little errors will continue to plague inquiring minds.

Address Histories

The first three basic identifiers answer the question, "Who?" Address histories tell you "Where" and "When." Knowing that a person lived all their adult life in the same community helps to focus a financial investigation. While such a person may own assets in other states, it is not probable. If a person has a wide-ranging address history, first place the addresses in chronological order. This timetable can tell an investigator if the subject had sufficient maturity and time to develop assets at the different locations.

For example, consider a twenty-four-year-old, currently working as a waiter, with five different addresses over the last five years in four different states. He probably does not have substantial property holdings elsewhere. However, do a careful second look at the California real estate and property holdings for a forty-five-year-old systems analyst, currently living in Texas, after twenty years in San Francisco. Coupled with other information resources, address histories can add a powerful logic to financial investigation.

COMMON SOURCES

The basic identifiers are not deep secrets, cloaked in extensive security. They exist in the public record; one needs only determination to find them. If you have a complete name for the subject, start at the local courthouse. If a full name is lacking, a bit of "trash research" may be necessary.

Trashing About

An individual's trash may blossom as a source of key identifiers. If the client knows where the subject lives, running by the house on trash day could reveal much new data. Bank statements, cancelled checks, credit card statements, billing statements, and business correspondence all can provide essential identifying data, especially when the correct names need discovering. The fine art of garbage browsing will receive attention in Chapter 5.

Voters' Registration

The Voters' Registration records should provide an investigator the full legal name of the subject, their current address, their DOB, and their social security number. In addition, by checking the alphabetical or geographical printouts, the investigator should find a similar listing for the subject's spouse. Some Voters' Registration files also contain the registrant's Place of Birth (POB) information. Be sure to make note of this little piece of data, especially if it is another city. If the rest of your inquiry indicates a large amount of assets, you may wish to check holdings that the subject may have in their former hometown.

Record Searching Techniques

Before going further, some insight into record-searching techniques may help. At the Voters' Registration office, for example, an investigator may encounter information in several formats:

1. The Public Computer Terminal.
2. Computer Printouts bound in volumes.
3. Microfiche.
4. The actual Registration Cards, filed in storage cabinets or bins.

Only the novice will consider these formats equivalent in what they offer the investigator. The Public Computer Terminal allows direct access to a single record quickly. One enters a subject's name; if the subject is a registrant, the data appears on the screen. But, if the database search software allows only single inquiries, you will miss seeing the subject's relatives who are also registrants. If the computer will not display a list of registrants with the same last name, you may need to consult the alphabetical or geographical computer printouts to find the relatives.

Looking at the computer printouts first may be helpful. However, keep in mind that the information found there is usually abbreviated or condensed. You may still have to examine the database, microfiche, or the cards themselves to obtain all the information. Yet, remember the geographical printout can assist in a special way: it acts as a crisscross directory for the subject's street. An investigator can use it to find neighbors for obtaining background information through telephone interviews.

Microfiche may contain images of the registration cards or of the computer printouts. It may be current or historical. The organization could be alphabetical, geographical, or chronological (by year of filing). Before using the microfiche, obtain assistance from the staff on its contents and organization. Since this medium is physically small, it is easier to look through than bulky printouts. However, you may need some help in learning to use the microfiche reader machine. Yet, when the line for using the computer terminals winds back to the front door, or if the stacks of printouts look forbidding, viewing microfiche may be an excellent alternative.

The actual registration cards contain all the information found in the other media. They also provide an exemplar of the subject's handwriting and signature which may be necessary for definitive identification later. The disadvantage of working with the original source document is that you may have to wade through a lot of paper to get to it. Yet, there are times when nothing else will do. A good rule to follow is always consult the original source document when in doubt on a crucial issue. Summaries and indexes do not tell the whole story.

TOOLS FOR ORGANIZING INFORMATION

Recognizing the respective power of different information media will become more vital to successful investigations as new technologies such as DVD and CD-ROM supplement existing resources. Richard

Saul Wurman in his book, *Information Anxiety,* argues that the information explosion of the late twentieth century offers us new ways to explore knowledge. Wurman says that five information tools exist to help organize data. We can organize information by:

1. Alphabet.
2. Location: Geography, Space, Position, or Place.
3. Time.
4. Category: Topic or Type.
5. Continuum: By Size or By Order.

An information source that offers all five of these tools as search methods is far richer than one which provides only alphabetical indexing. The Voters' Registration records utilize, for example, three methods of access: alphabetical, by location, and by time (historical). Considering the avenues of access a source creates new perspectives on analyzing information.

The Telephone Book

One simple source, overlooked as an investigative tool, is the telephone book. A quick review of its holdings, using Wurman's principles, may expand our understanding of what he is trying to communicate. The telephone book lists names alphabetically without regard to location within a municipality. One has to know two pieces of information to find a telephone number: the correct full name and the town or city where the person lives. If the name is a common one, knowing the street address would help find the person out of a long list of names. The possession of telephone directories covering several years adds a time search capability. An investigator could trace an address history of an individual using this historical collection. Perhaps it could also identify the subject's relatives.

The Yellow Pages provide categorical searches since they list businesses, products, and services by topic. Placing large urban telephone books on CD-ROM enables one to search by name (alphabet), by street address (location), by year (time), and by topic (category). Combined searches are also possible: all the John Jones listed as barbers in Houston, Texas in 1991.

Placing statewide telephone books on CD-ROM would be even more powerful. Name searches become feasible without knowing the specific town or city. The disc could even offer continuum searches. One could request all the John Q. Jones in Texas. The search software would print out on the screen a list of all the cities that had the name listing. By displaying the city with the greatest number of listings at the beginning, the continuum would go down to the city with the least number at the bottom. Beside each city's name would be the number of listings.

This brief discussion of the five information tools casts a wider perspective on the problems of accessing data. Often, the answer stares you right in the face; getting to it is the challenge. Attacking access problems using different media and search strategies is the main theme of this book.

COURTHOUSE FILES

Courthouse criminal files often provide DOB, SSN, address, and full-name information either on the personal bond application or on the arrest affidavit. Also, supplementary documents in the file created by the sheriff's office, police department, probation office, and county or district clerk may contain these identifiers. Searching on the clerk's database may produce either a list of people with the same surname or a direct hit. Become familiar with the capabilities of the system; evaluate the types of searches possible. Consider the possibility that the subject's relatives may have criminal files too; hence, the computer-generated surname list may deserve scrutiny.

Civil Court Records

Civil lawsuit and probate records may contain key identifiers. Be sure to read through the pleadings and discovery documents such as Answers to Interrogatories and Responses to Request for Production. Interrogatories are written questions posed by one party to another in a lawsuit. They frequently ask the full name, address, DOB, and SSN of the person responding. Requests for Production require a party in a lawsuit to provide copies of documents relevant to the proceedings. These documents may include medical bills and records, lost wage information, and so on. Many of these types of documents will contain key identifiers.

The pleadings themselves (petitions and motions) and any depositions (questioning under oath) taken may also contain personal identifiers. Routinely checking names for civil actions becomes easier each day as more court clerks automate their indexes with computer terminals and databases. Learn how to use your local courts' databases and integrate the searches as a regular part of your casework. Your investigations will benefit greatly.

OTHER COMMON SOURCES

Driver's license records can supply DOB and, in some states, SSN information. Address information is also a part of the record. Requesting a copy of the original application for a driver's license will possibly tell you a previous address and other personal information like place of birth (POB). Finding out when the license was last renewed or updated can indicate how valid the current address may be. Traffic accidents and tickets recorded on the driving history can lead to police reports and court files. These sources will reveal associates, relatives, and addresses.

City crisscrosses or directories allow you to search by location for name or by name for an address. Additionally, reverse searching by telephone numbers is possible. These reference works provide historical information. Usually, a small date appears by the person's name indicating when they first entered the directory at that location. Many historical centers at public libraries have directories covering a span of years. They provide an excellent source for researching address history. The same centers also offer collections of past telephone books and utility microfiche.

LESSER KNOWN SOURCES

Perhaps the most overlooked sources for background information on individuals and businesses are newspaper and periodical databases. Extensive discussion on their uses as investigative tools will occur later in Chapter 3. Meanwhile, they serve as quick sources of basic identifier leads for the savvy investigator. Rarely do exact dates of birth or social security numbers appear about a subject in the press. However, in news stories, especially those dealing with criminal activities, one finds the names, addresses, and ages of those arrested. Such stories lead to finding the criminal file or the agency that can supply more specific information. Even articles on business or human interest concerns convey valuable information concerning a subject's full name, other addresses, the ownership of businesses, relatives, and associates.

Searching by name on the local newspaper's CD-ROM database can yield extensive biographical data on a subject. These CD-ROM discs are becoming available for more newspapers all the time. University or large public libraries are making these resources open to the public. If your local newspaper is not yet on CD-ROM, check with the local history center at the public library to see if they create their own in-house index. They may be able to do searches for you. The newspaper itself may have a computerized index that it makes available to the public.

The local police database may provide limited access to the public. In Texas, the public portion of an incident report is available. It may contain all of the basic identifiers on an individual. Name searches with a specified time range permit scanning of the database for any incidents involving your subject. Check with your local police department on procedures and on the extent of searches available.

The municipal court database will have identifier data on individuals charged with traffic tickets and lesser misdemeanors. These documents will supply name, DOB, address, driver's license, and license plate numbers. In areas that are not urbanized, generally a justice of the peace (JP) or similar court will have the same types of files. These lesser courts can be information treasure chests. Normally, investigators like to head for the "high country" of the district or county courts. Do not forget the gold in the foothills of the municipal and JP courts.

FINANCIAL STATEMENTS

Financial statements obtained from previous landlords, finance companies, bankruptcy filings, banks, state licensing agencies, or even bail bond companies reveal extensive financial and personal identifying data. (A financial statement lists personal information like the full name, address, and SSN along with the assets, liabilities, income, and expenses of the subject. Either the subject or their accountant prepares the statement to gain financing or governmental approval.) An investigator will find the number of these statements floating around to be surprising. Financial institutions, attorneys, and collections people trying to recover money from the same subject may share with you. Often, if you have information to trade, getting what others know is not that difficult. Learn to think like a trader when seeking financial details.

PROFESSIONAL DIRECTORIES

If your subject is a professional person, they probably will be listed in some kind of professional directory. You will find good biographical information, including DOB, about lawyers in the *Martindale-Hubbell Law Directory*. There are numerous similar directories supplying basic biographical and address data for medical doctors. Check with your local university librarian. Directories exist for almost every conceivable profession or occupation. If finding the name of a relevant professional directory becomes a problem, consult *Directories in Print* at your local library. Biographical reference works such as the *Who's Who* series or *Biography and Genealogy Master Index* may provide valuable background on professionals or prominent persons.

Special historical collections contain everything from telephone books to cemetery plot indexes. The rule of thumb is to head for your local collection when you need to build an extensive address history. Another time to consider the local special collections is when a gap occurs in the present-day record. You know your target works as an interior designer, but they are not listed in the current state or national directories of interior designers. The reason for this could be one of many: they did not pay their dues on time; they did not like the organization anymore; the organization did not receive the biography form in time; the list goes on. However, a past directory may contain complete biographical information with identifiers that are still reasonably accurate. Your local historical collection with old directories may fill in such gaps.

GOVERNMENTAL RECORDS

State licensing and regulatory agencies will have either DOB or SSN data on applications. In many cases, they will have both. Additionally, the files will contain the full name and address of the applicant. For information on the types of permits and licenses issued in a given state, consult the respective state governmental manual. These manuals identify all the state agencies and explain the regulatory duties of each. Also, examining the blue governmental pages of the telephone book under State Government will supply a quick overview.

Death certificates contain SSN and DOB information along with the full name of the deceased. If investigating the assets of a deceased person, checking at the state's repository for vital records will require the full name and the date of death. However, coupled with a stop at county probate court, the death certificate can tell the investigator a great deal about the names of relatives.

Routinely running subjects' names on the database at Bankruptcy Court makes sense. Even if the target has not filed bankruptcy, they may be a creditor in a bankruptcy case. As a creditor, they will have documents on file which may contain the key identifiers. Bankruptcy files provide large quantities of financial information about debtors and sometimes creditors. We will discuss them at length in Chapter 3.

SUMMARY

The top sources for personal identifiers are:

• Driver's License Records
• Civil and Probate Records
• Bankruptcy Court
• Death Certificates
• Courthouse Criminal Files
• Voters' Registration
• Trash
• Police and Municipal Court Databases
• Professional Directories
• City Crisscrosses

In using information resources, it is important to search for data utilizing as many of the five information tools as possible. Remember that information can be organized by: alphabet, time, location, category, or continuum. These tools involve looking at the same data from different perspectives. These new perspectives may help you uncover facts that were not apparent before.

Chapter 2

IDENTIFYING RELATIVES AND ASSOCIATES

Approach asset investigation with a roving eye, looking to the left and the right, as well as straight ahead. This way of seeing will enhance the quality of your work product. Learn to think about who has the money and where it may be. If someone earns $90,000 a year but has nothing in their own name, start by assuming, to borrow from Sherlock Holmes, that some kind of "game is afoot." What names are the assets in? Why does this subject wish to appear judgment-proof now? How long has he or she been preparing for the invasion of the debt collectors? This chapter presents some of the basic techniques for acquiring the "other names." Hopefully, the ideas offered will prevent you from having to grope endlessly through a fog of unknown personalities and alliances.

BASIC SOURCES

The complexity of financial investigation requires that any inquiry must first uncover all of the "players." Simply checking public records only by the name of the target business or individual will not do. Adding the names of the business's officers to the search is an improvement. However, what if assets are placed in the name of the officer's spouse, son, or daughter? How will you locate them? Avoid narrow tunnel vision, focusing on only the initial targeted names; instead, broaden your inquiry to acquire the names of relatives, friends, and associates. Businesses do not exist in a vacuum. Few individuals live in isolation. Seek out the ties, connections, and links.

What are the sources for a subject's relatives, friends, associates, and business affiliations? One may first wish to look at the subject's driver's license file. If their driving record produces any automobile accidents, obtain the police report for each. These reports may contain the names of vehicle owners or passengers connected to the subject. Polk's applicable city directory generally has employment or occupational descriptions and the names of other family members with each individual listing. In checking a subject's criminal records at the courthouse, one usually finds the names of friends and relatives on personal bond applications.

Motor Vehicle Address Searches

Running a subject's motor vehicle registration or driver's license *using an address methodology* can produce a list of all licensees and registrants living with the subject. An investigator can run, for example, 1111 John Paul Jones Blvd. in Timbuktu, Texas and find out John Q. Public owns a 1988 Chevrolet there, along with Mary Q. Public's 1987 Ford and John Q. Public, Jr.'s 1989 Buick. Many information brokers (see Chap. 4) provide this type of search at reasonable rates.

Another document to check at the DMV is the subject's Original License Application. This application usually contains the name and driver's license number of a sponsoring parent. From this information an investigator can locate the county of residence for the surviving parent. If a property search of that county reveals real estate owned by the parents, your client can file an Abstract of Judgment there. If the subject inherits the property, your client may be able to collect the judgment off of that land.

The Local Newspaper on CD-ROM

With the advent of CD-ROM technology more local newspapers offer full-text searching by name. For example, where I live in Austin, Texas, the University of Texas's central library has a CD-ROM of the *Austin American-Statesman* for the last two years. With the successful running of individual names on the database, I learned the names of associates and relatives, employers, about their criminal arrests, and the birth announcements of subjects" children.

Since papers like the *American-Statesman* frequently run profiles of local businesses and their owners, CD-ROM searches are a good bet in almost any financial investigation. They enable one to do effective parallel background research on both an individual and their business interests. Another powerful tool is the Secretary of State's office in your jurisdiction. A subject's name run on the Officer/Director database in the Corporations Division could reveal employment or ownership in businesses previously unknown.

Other Miscellaneous Sources

As District and County Clerks become more computerized, routinely running a subject's name on both civil and criminal indexes may provide files yielding employment and other vital background information. County Clerks are providing easier access by computer terminal to miscellaneous public records such as Assumed Name Filings, Military Discharges, County UCC Filings, Tax Liens, and Alcoholic Beverage Licenses. Centralized searches by subject's name are now feasible and could yield extensive background or occupational information.

A check of Voter's Registration records could reveal employment information in certain states. These records are also an excellent way of determining the identity of the subject's spouse and other live-in relatives.

OTHER STATES AND LOCALITIES

If you feel that your subject has business involvement in other states or localities, scan national databases of newspapers such as DataTimes, NEXIS/LEXIS, the National Newspaper Index (InfoTrac), and Newsbank Electronic Index. A good place to start accessing these databases is the local college or university library.

Another useful service is OCLC (Online Computer Library Center) which contains an index to college library catalogues nationwide. Using OCLC recently, I was able to locate a book written by a subject and, from the bibliographic data, to determine he worked as an anthropologist with a Texas university. Name searches on OCLC are fairly easy. Enter the first four letters of the last name and the first initial. That will usually lead to a hit. OCLC is an excellent resource when a subject may be a published author. If the person comes from a family of authors or academics, OCLC can uncover the relatives. (It is important to note that a published book may be paying royalties to the subject.)

Another similar database, available at many university libraries, is RLIN (Research Libraries Information System). Either resource offers ready access when research collections exist on an individual, their family, or business.

Do not overlook historical sources of occupational or background information. In Austin, for example, the public library maintains an historical collection of Austin telephone books, city directories, and crisscrosses. Such a collection can tell you how long someone has worked at a particular place or operated a business there.

Also, if a current directory does not supply job information or family ties, maybe a previous one will. For other cities in Texas, the University of Texas at Austin has a telephone directory collection at the Center for American History. I recently used this collection to calculate how long a doctor had been practicing medicine in an East Texas town. Building a chronology from the progression of telephone directories was easy. A timeline constructed from the chronology enabled us to tell when other doctors entered and left the targeted physician's practice. An investigator should find comparable historical resources in any major city.

CDB Infotek provides access to comprehensive public records from many states. The system allows integrated, multi-state searches of bankruptcy, judgment, tax lien, UCC, and corporate information. Name searches can reveal a subject's business involvement in other jurisdictions. Universal searches by name of all files in all states on the database are possible. (Using the system requires a subscription by calling the customer service number at 1-800-333-8356.)

Many information brokers and vendors offer Interstate (or Intrastate) Public Filings (IPF). These records cover lawsuits, tax liens, and bankruptcies over several states. Generally, the charges are on a per-case basis. IPF's value lies in locating a subject's business interests in other jurisdictions.

Information brokers also provide what is known as credit header searching. A person's credit file contains two parts. The first is the so-called "public section" which has the person's address history and social security number. The second is the actual credit history which is confidential except for the exemptions granted under the Fair Credit Reporting Act (FCRA). When one has the subject's SSN, searching all of the national credit databases to locate header information on other residences is easy. From this search one can uncover leads to finding relatives, businesses, and assets in other jurisdictions. (I will offer ideas about locating information brokers, along with a discussion of the FCRA, later in Chapter 4.)

MAILING LISTS

Mailing list providers provide databases of prospective customers broken down by income, age, profession, geography, economic status of neighborhood, and so on. A list offers leads about a subject's neighbors and relatives. Working with the provider to do name scans of the database should uncover relatives. Knowing the economic status of neighbors should help judge that of the subject. One local provider in Austin keeps track of persons who purchase expensive automobiles by paying cash. Consider the other imaginative possibilities in database searching using mailing lists. The Yellow Pages in Austin have advertisements with wording similar to AMERICAN BUSINESS LISTS– 1.3 million high income Americans listed or AUSTIN TRAVIS COUNTY DIRECTORY–275,000 Austin residences updated monthly. Contact the providers in your area to gain access to this unusual source of financial intelligence.

SECURITIES AND EXCHANGE COMMISSION (SEC)

Disclosure/Spectrum Database offers full-text searches of the SEC filings of over five thousand publicly owned companies. When a subject is a major player in the business world, this is a top-notch source for uncovering their involvement. The data could lead to discovering the names of associates and relatives. It is available through DIALOG and through major university libraries. Also at university libraries, CD-ROM databases such as ABI/INFORM or SEC ONLINE allow access to the names of officers and key shareholders of major American businesses.

SOCIAL SECURITY NUMBER

An investigator may utilize the numbering system of the social security number to learn the home state of a subject. The first three numbers form a prefix which identifies the issuing state. An index to the first three digits of the SSN appears in Table 1.

The full number serves as a locating device. Information brokers

Table 1
SOCIAL SECURITY NUMBER PREFIXES

001-003	New Hampshire	501-502	North Dakota
004-007	Maine	503-504	South Dakota
008-009	Vermont	505-508	Nebraska
010-034	Massachusetts	509-515	Kansas
035-039	Rhode Island	516-517	Montana
040-049	Connecticut	518-519	Idaho
050-134	New York	520	Wyoming
135-158	New Jersey	521-524	Colorado
159-211	Pennsylvania	525	New Mexico
212-220	Maryland	526-527	Arizona
221-222	Delaware	528-529	Utah
223-231	Virginia	530	Nevada
232-236	West Virginia	531-539	Washington
237-246	North Carolina	540-544	Oregon
247-251	South Carolina	545-573	California
252-260	Georgia	574	Alaska
261-267	Florida	575-576	Hawaii
268-302	Ohio	577-579	D.C.
303-317	Indiana	580	Virgin Islands
318-361	Illinois	580-584	Puerto Rico
362-386	Michigan	585	New Mexico
387-399	Wisconsin	586	Guam and Samoa
400-415	Tennessee	587-588	Mississippi
416-424	Alabama	589-591	Florida
425-428	Mississippi	592-595	Florida
429-432	Arkansas	596-599	Puerto Rico
433-439	Louisiana	600-601	Arizona
440-448	Oklahoma	602-626	California
449-467	Texas	627-699	Unassigned
468-477	Minnesota	700-728	Railroad Retirement
478-485	Iowa	729-999	Unassigned
486-500	Missouri		

offer searches using the SSN. These searches can provide a list of places where the subject lived before. Checking the home state for birth records will uncover the parents' names. A search for marriage and birth records in states where the subject previously resided can produce the names of the spouse and the subject's children. This type of search becomes easier at the county level due to the increasing automation of clerk's records.

HUMAN SOURCES

Driving by the subject's house in the evening hours may provide license plate numbers of friends and associates. Interviewing neighbors may reveal information about the subject's acquaintances. If you learn the subject is active in a neighborhood association, club, or sports group, attending a meeting could identify the person's inner circle. Local businesses such as shops, restaurants, taverns, bowling lanes, and pool halls may be places to observe the subject with associates. Do not overlook persons who make deliveries to the home on a regular basis. The pizza delivery person, the cable television installer, the newspaper delivery person, the mail handler, and the swimming pool cleaner all may have something to tell you.

Other creditors may share with you copies of loan applications containing references to relatives, friends, and associates. If collection agencies show activity on the subject's credit file, checking with them may reveal references given by the subject when first obtaining credit. Or, they may share what they learned about the subject during their own investigation.

Interviewing the former landlord could be profitable. Inside information on relatives and associates may be available on the rental application. If the apartment complex has an active tenants association, an officer may tell you useful information about the target's circle of friends and relatives.

The subject's membership in public service organizations such as the Red Cross, volunteer fire department, police or sheriff's reserve unit, or neighborhood watch group may lead to persons with useful knowledge. Participation in a church group or charitable organization may provide people with a knowledge of the subject's social circle.

Learning the professional or trade organization where the subject belongs could lead to members who know the person. The source of this information may be news articles in the general or business press. A profile of the subject in a trade magazine could also clue one in. Or, perhaps the Yellow Pages will have an ad on the subject's business which lists professional associations. Attending meetings of the group could lead to useful background information. Interviewing the group's officers may be beneficial.

Newspaper accounts or inputs from human sources may identify cultural, literary, or civic groups the subject participates in. The local community theater group, civic chorus, or local orchestra may provide people who have in-depth knowledge about your subject and his or her ties to others. The subject's family may be major donators or patrons to the group. Again, the officers of the organization may be able to fill you in on the details.

SUMMARY

Learning about the circle of relatives and associates "orbiting" the target requires imagination and dogged investigative effort. One can consult public record sources such as the local newspaper index, birth certificates, driver's license records, marriage licenses, and databases like CDB Infotek or Interstate Public Filings. Social security numbers can lead to the home town or state of a subject and to previous addresses around the nation.

Finally, human sources such as neighbors, other members of clubs and professional organizations, and operators of neighborhood businesses can enlighten the investigator on the subject's social background. The art of asset investigation requires this integration of public and private sources to obtain the total picture.

Use Form 1 to record the information developed on the subject's relatives and associates.

Form 1

Subject's Pedigree

Case: Date:

Subject:

Aliases: Maiden Name:

Mother: Grandparents:

Father:

Spouses: In-Laws:

Children:

Sisters/Brothers:

Cousins/Nephews/Nieces:

Friends and Associates:

Business Associates:

Extramarital or Premarital: Any Children:

Form 1

Continued

Checklist:

Local Newspaper Scan [ ]

Court Records [ ]

IPF or Prentice Hall (CDB Infotek) [ ]

OCLC or RLIN [ ]

DIALOG, ABI/INFORM, SEC ONLINE, or InfoTrac [ ]

NEXIS/LEXIS [ ]

Vital Records [ ]

Voter's Registration [ ]

Driver's License [ ]

Historical [ ]

Yellow Pages [ ]

Credit Header [ ]

Criminal Records [ ]

SSN Chart [ ]

Crisscross [ ]

Mailing Lists [ ]

Human Sources [ ]

Internet Search Engines for Web Sites [ ]   For Newsgroups [ ]

Chapter 3

BASIC SOURCES FOR INDIVIDUALS

This chapter will cover the basic sources that should be a part of any individual asset search. Proper searching at this level will insure effective inquiry at the advanced stage. The basic sources include:

1. Legal databases and Civil Lawsuit indexes.
2. Probate court records.
3. Bankruptcy court.
4. Vehicle databases and records.
5. Aircraft records.
6. Uniform Commercial Code filings.
7. Tax Liens.
8. Corporate filings (Officer/Director).
9. Real Property records.
10. Criminal and Driver's License records (if not done already to establish identifiers as indicated in Chapter 1.)

The chapter will also describe some of the various databases useful in financial investigation. NEXIS/LEXIS is a family of newspaper and legal databases provided by Mead Data Central in Dayton, Ohio. It is available through information brokers, large universities, and state-run libraries. WESTLAW provides access to most of the current case law in the United States. Owned by West Publishing, it is found in law libraries and in many lawyers' offices. Like NEXIS/LEXIS, WESTLAW access takes place by modem from a personal computer. Additionally, WESTLAW offers state and regional cases on CD-ROM for use on a personal computer.

National Newspaper Index, Legal Resource Index, and InfoTrac are all services of Information Access Company which indexes newspaper, legal, and general magazine articles. University and large public libraries provide these databases on terminals or at personal computers for in-house use.

DataTimes is a commercial database of newspapers from around the country. It is available through some information brokers or by direct subscription. CDB Infotek and Information America provide access to public records such as UCC filings, lawsuits, and corporate filings in key states around the U.S.A. Direct subscription is possible.

OCLC and RLIN are indexes to major college and university library holdings across the nation. University and major research libraries provide access to these databases. ABI/INFORM is a database of magazine articles about industry and business. It is available on CD-ROM at many university libraries.

THE LAW SPEAKS

An investigator should not overlook an individual's involvement with the legal system. Databases such as LEXIS, WESTLAW, and Legal Resource Index provide information on criminal and civil cases, requiring an appeal, in which the target possibly was a party. Additionally, if a case involved press coverage or an article in a legal journal, then Legal Resource Index would be an excellent source.

Checking the microfiche at the Federal District Clerk's Office may reveal civil, criminal, or, best of all, bankruptcy cases involving the subject. Even if the subject is a *creditor* in a bankruptcy, the file will contain valuable initial business and occupational information.

With the advent of centralized computer indexes, civil cases (which include divorce actions) are a remarkable source of financial information. Divorce cases may contain documents showing division of property. Finding financial statements and lists of assets are common. Accident cases could have occupational, educational, and income data supplied in response to interrogatories or requests for production.

Even when subjects are not a parties to a lawsuit, their depositions may disclose valuable background material. While no index to witnesses exists at the District Clerk's office, the subject may be a known expert witness who testifies regularly. (Running the subject's name on WESTLAW, LEXIS/NEXIS, or the local newspaper's database may help uncover "the frequent testifier.") Or, checking with area attorneys may provide the necessary lead that a subject testified in a certain case. If the deposition is not in the clerk's file, the court reporter or the opposing lawyer could supply a copy.

Other ideas concerning civil records include:

1. Be on the lookout for "sweetheart lawsuits." Mr. Jones borrows heavily from creditors. He does not wish to repay, so he has a friend, Ms. Smith, sue him. No answer is filed, and Ms. Smith takes a big default judgment. When Mr. Jones files the bankruptcy, a large portion of the liquidated bankruptcy estate goes to Ms. Smith. Guess what? Ms. Smith returns the money to Mr. Jones after taking out her handling fee. (More concerning this later in Chapter 7 about hidden assets.)

2. Try to identify enemies and adversaries of the subject from the court records. They could prove useful when doing advanced levels of investigation.

3. Run separately the names of key persons found in the lawsuit's documents against newspaper databases such as your local newspaper on CD-ROM, NEXIS/LEXIS, National Newspaper Index, DataTimes, or Newsbank. And then, do the same on the court clerk's computerized index. This collateral type of inquiry could produce relationships, between your subject and others, not recognized before.

4. Any references to other lawsuits in the one-at-hand should be investigated. They may produce additional background or financial insight on the subject.

5. Be sure to cross-check clerks' indexes at the Federal District Court, State District Court, and State County Court levels. You may discover "sweetheart lawsuits" and other hidden connections this way. If one finds a case that underwent an appeal, then check the records at the appeals court, or use NEXIS/LEXIS or WESTLAW, to locate the outcome.

6. CDB Infotek can find judgments in other jurisdictions. The same goes for Interstate Public Filings and Business Public Filings, both available through information brokers. Also, one should not overlook Legal Resource Index, Business Periodical Index, ABI/INFORM, and InfoTrac for press or magazine coverage of litigation involving your target.

7. When you know the names of the parents, checking the probate records under those names may lead to discovering an inheritance by the subject.

BANKRUPTCY RECORDS

These records are a treasure of information. An investigator learns a great deal about the finances of an individual by carefully studying the court file. The main components of the file consist of:

1. Proof of Claim forms filed by creditors, indicating the amount of debt owed to them.

2. Creditor Matrix. (A list of all the creditors.)

3. Trustee's Final Report and Account. (The court-appointed trustee's report which explains what action they took in the case and what funds were disbursed to which creditors.)

4. Orders of the court.

5. Motions before the court.

6. Chapter 13 or Chapter 7 Plan Summary. (The plan for resolving the creditors' claims filed by the debtor. Chapter 13 is a plan to repay the creditors under court supervision. Chapter 7 is a complete liquidation of the bankruptcy estate which terminates the creditors' claims.)

7. Schedule A–Real Property. (Lists all real property owned by the debtor.)

8. Schedule B–Personal Property.

9. Schedule C–Property Claimed as Exempt. (Lists all property that the debtor feels is exempt from liquidation under the law.)

10. Schedule D–Creditors Holding Secured Claims.

11. Schedule E–Creditors Holding Unsecured Priority Claims. (Lists creditors such as persons owed wages and governmental units owed taxes who are ahead in the line, by law, of non-priority unsecured creditors such as credit card companies.)

12. Schedule F–Creditors Holding Unsecured Non-Priority Claims.

13. Schedule G–Executory Contracts and Unexpired Leases.

14. Schedule H–Co-Debtors.

15. Schedule I–Current Income of Individual Debtors. (A current cash flow or income statement.)

16. Schedule J–Current Expenditures of Individual Debtors. (A current cash outflow or expense statement.)

17. Summary of Schedules. (Summarizes schedules A through J.)

18. Summary of Financial Affairs. (Explains all the major financial events leading up to bankruptcy. It is mainly used to detect last

minute reallocations of assets and profligate spending.)

19.　Statement of Attorney Compensation. (How much the debtor is paying his or her attorney who prepared the bankruptcy.)

20.　Chapter 13 or 7 Plan. (The detailed account by the debtor on how the creditors' claims are to be resolved.)

21.　Transcripts of any Proceedings or Depositions.

22.　Transcript of the 205A Examination. (A lawyer representing the creditors interviews the debtor to determine if fraud is a factor in the bankruptcy.)

In addition to the clerk's records, if the suspicion of fraud exists, one may check with the Office of United States Trustee to see if they ever conducted a fraud investigation. Normally, at the conclusion of a case, the Trustee's Report is deposited in the clerk's file. If a case is closed and then stored in the regional warehouse, an investigator can order a complete copy for a relatively small fee.

In possible bankruptcy fraud cases, the warning signs are:

a.　*The Use of Shell Corporations.*　An individual or company owns more than one business. Of these businesses, one acts as the vehicle for incurring debts. Meanwhile, the other company or companies receive the goods and services purchased on credit. The debt vehicle ends up in bankruptcy court while the other businesses make huge profits on free goods.

b.　*Loan-to-Cash Schemes.*　Buy a business with a loan. Sell off the assets of the business for cash. Then, place the business in bankruptcy with the sob story to the lender that you "tried to make a go of it."

c.　*Sweetheart Lawsuits.*

d.　*A History of Businesses in Bankruptcy.*　An individual has a track record of corporate but not personal bankruptcy. In fact, the individual personally lives quite well.

Discovering these abuses will require cross-checking Officer/ Director records, civil court indexes, UCC filings, and articles in the business press. If the individual or business had glowing reviews in the local business press just months or a year before the bankruptcy, start interviewing. Talk to former employees, lending officers, collections personnel, and business journalists. You may be able to collect enough evidence to rule out a legitimate financial failure.

OCCUPATIONAL INFORMATION

A subject's occupation generally governs their earning capacity, which in turn produces assets: savings, investments, cars, boats, real estate, and so on. What are the sources for a subject's job or self-employment information? If an automobile accident occurred, the police report may state it. Polk's applicable city directory generally has employment or occupational descriptions with individual listings. In checking criminal records at the courthouse, one usually finds employment information on personal bond applications filled out by a subject. Running a subject's motor vehicle registration can produce lienholder data which could identify an employer-sponsored institution such as General Electric or IBM Employees Credit Union.

With the advent of CD-ROM technology more local newspapers offer full-text searching by name. As indicated earlier, the CD-ROM of the *Austin American-Statesman* produces employment data frequently by searching for individual names.

Since papers like the *American-Statesman* often run profiles of local businesses and their owners, CD-ROM searches are a good bet in almost any financial investigation. They enable one to do effective background research on both individuals and their business interests. Another powerful tool is the Secretary of State's office in your jurisdiction. A subject's name run on the Officer/Director database in the Corporations Division could reveal employment or ownership in businesses previously unknown.

As District and County Clerks become more computerized, routinely running a subject's name on both civil and criminal indexes may provide files yielding employment and other vital background information. County Clerks are providing easier access by computer terminal to miscellaneous public records such as Assumed Name Filings, Military Discharges, County UCC Filings, Tax Liens, and Alcoholic Beverage Licenses. Centralized searches by subject's name are now feasible and could yield occupational information.

A check of Voter's Registration records could reveal employment information in certain states. These records are an excellent way of determining the identity of the subject's spouse. Then doing a parallel investigation of the spouse's employment will make your search far more accurate and complete.

VEHICLES

Perhaps the most effective database search is of motor vehicle records by the subject's name. Some information brokers refer to this type of inquiry as an "alpha search" (by alphabetical listing as opposed to by license plate number). It generally produces a list of all vehicles registered to an individual in the state. As indicated previously, this search not only adds to the list of assets owned by the subject, but it may also reveal the location of other assets statewide.

Lienholder information obtained may offer insight into the subject's banking connections. Also, creditworthiness may be calculated from the lien dates on the titles and the number of vehicles successfully paid off–for example, if a subject buys a BMW and a Lincoln Town car in 1987 and 1988, respectively, and he still owns them in 1993 when he purchases a 1993 Mercury Sable. If he is using the same lienholder, then his creditworthiness speaks for itself. On the other hand, if someone has a title date (when they originally purchased the vehicle) of 12-13-91 and a lien date (when a lien came into being) of 2-15-93, then this may be a sign of financial trouble. They probably had to use an unencumbered asset as collateral for an emergency loan.

Record lienholder data gathered from motor vehicle registrations on the Banking Summary (see Chapter 11) and on the Individual Summary (see Form 2). When the analysis stage comes into play, this information will be readily available for correlation with other banking data.

BOATS

In Texas, the Parks and Wildlife Department maintains a database of boat registrations by registration number and by name of owner. The number for the Texas Parks and Wildlife boat database is 512-389-4828. A live operator will do the search for you. The only time they have problems on name searches is with common last names such as Smith or Jones. Having complete name information helps in such situations. Unfortunately, the TPW does not currently have the facilities for off-site modem access to the database.

In addition to contacting the department directly, an investigator may do alpha searches through Texas-based information brokers. The information on the printout will include the boat's length, year built and model year, the manufacturer's identification number, the serial number, type of hull, means of propulsion and fuel used, use of boat, and any liens. Much like alpha searches on motor vehicle records, this database can provide evidence of financial activity in other counties. One should integrate the boat's lienholder information with the other banking data.

For locating boat registration databases in other states, one may consult the reference book, *State Administrative Officials Classified by Function 1991-1992,* published by The Council of State Governments (Lexington, Kentucky 1991). It is available in public libraries and lists all of the various state agencies that administer the boat registration laws. Of course, information brokers (IBs) in other states may be able to provide direct database access.

Several reference works on boats and yachts are useful:

1. *BUC's New Boat Price Guide* by BUC International Corporation (1-800-327-6929, Ft. Lauderdale, FL) lists new price information.

2. *BUC's Used Boat Price Guide.*

3. *Register of American Yachts,* 1991, by Yacht Owners Register, Inc. (617-536-9222, Boston, MA.) lists over 30,000 yachts by owner. A valuable book if researching an affluent subject.

4. *Directories in Print 1993,* 10th edition, Charles B. Montney, editor, Gale Research. This work, found at public libraries, lists many directories about boating and boats. In fact, if an investigator needs a lead on almost any topic, this is the book to consult. More discussion about the uses for this book will occur later in the text.

AIRCRAFT

National Aircraft Title searches, by either owner's name or by N-Number, are available through information brokers around the country. The database printout will include:

1. N-number
2. Serial number, manufacturer's name and model
3. Aircraft and engine type
4. Year of manufacture
5. Owner's name and address
6. Certification date

However, any lienholder information will be missing. The Federal Aviation Administration does not list lienholder information on its database because of the extensive computer storage required. The remedy is to call the Aircraft Registration Branch at 405-954-3116 and to request a title search. After supplying an N-Number and your mailing address to the A.R.B., you will receive a microfiche from them by mail. It will contain any lien instruments placed on the title. They will bill for the nominal cost of the fiche. Be sure to record any lienholder data in the banking section of the provided forms.

Another source of title information on aircraft is the *United States Civil Aircraft Registry,* a microfiche of basic title information on over 275,000 aircraft. It is published monthly by Insured Aircraft Title Service, Inc. (800-654-4882 or 800477-4882, Oklahoma City, OK).

ABD-Aviation Buyer's Directory, published by Air Service Directory, Inc. (203-325-2647, Stamford, CT), covers aircraft, parts, and equipment manufacturers. Coming out quarterly at 400 pages, it can be a useful tool for locating experts on aircraft prices and values.

UCC FILINGS

Uniform Commercial Code filings, with the exception of tax liens, normally do not contain the dollar value of the loan or the collateral pledged for the loan. They are of interest to the financial investigator because they do document:

1. The name and address of the lender (secured party).
2. Date of the loan.
3. A description of the pledged collateral, including sometimes the purchase order number and the serial numbers of the equipment involved.
4. Persons signing the instrument on behalf of the secured party and the debtor.

The UCC filing helps to determine the outstanding liabilities of an individual and the secured assets that they may possess. In addition, the filing answers the question, When did the individual acquire the asset? It also serves to document who in a business has the authority to place it in debt. A signature on a UCC filing will establish that an individual is in fact an officer of that business. Finally, the UCC filing may establish the identity of an individual's bank. One may even have the name of the bank officer to call for "reference information."

One may deduce from the various UCC documents other valuable information that may be on file:

- Original financing statement, or continuation of O.F.S.
- Amendments.
- Partial release of collateral
- Assignment or subordination

Placing these documents in a chronological sequence may help an investigator understand the financial evolution of an individual or business. Why did the loan get continued? How did the individual manage a lump sum partial payoff of the debt? Why did they acquire this piece of equipment now? Asking such questions will greatly enhance your investigative work product. Since UCC filings exist at both the county and state level, search the databases of the county clerk's office and the Secretary of State's office in your jurisdiction. NEXIS/LEXIS' Lien Library, Information America, and CDB Infotek are also sources of UCC filings.

TAX LIENS

State and local tax liens appear on the records at the county clerk's office. With new computerized databases running, an individual's name becomes easy. More and more, clerk's offices offer integrated searches of tax liens along with other records such as assumed name filings and hospital liens. Federal tax liens may be found at both the county and at the Secretary of State's office. To detect tax liens from other jurisdictions, use CDB Infotek, Information America, or Interstate Public Filings through your information broker. Once an investigator has the basic tax lien data, a call to the proper taxing authority may yield further information.

Tax liens are a big solid negative in the liability column. Usually, individuals try to get them removed as soon as possible. They can be a real stumbling block to creditworthiness. However, just because someone has a tax lien does not mean that they are insolvent, or that they have not made payment arrangements. Analyze any tax liens in the context of an individual's overall financial situation. Avoid making quick assumptions.

CORPORATIONS: OFFICER/DIRECTOR

Running any subjects' name on the Officer/Director database of corporate records at the Secretary of State in your jurisdiction can be very profitable. Unveiling the ownership or control of a business is the goal. To do similar searches on a nationwide basis, use a private information vendor such as CDB Infotek or Information America.

After locating a company in which your subject is an officer, looking at the actual corporate file may be valuable. The articles of incorporation contain the name of the incorporators, possibly the corporate counsel's name and address, sometimes the names of principal stockholders, and general organizational information. The file should be available for inspection at the Secretary of State's office.

If the company is publicly owned, further information may be on Disclosure/Spectrum which is on DIALOG. Also, one may search SEC ONLINE, a CD-ROM database. An investigator should not ignore checking ABI/INFORM, Business Periodical Index, and InfoTrac for articles leading to profile information on the company.

A check with the corporate taxing authority in your state could reveal what tax permits and accounts the business has in effect. For example, an investigator could learn in what counties the business has sales tax permits and if the business is current on its corporation taxes. In a case where we tried to learn in which Texas counties a hotel chain operated, checking the Hotel Tax records at the Comptroller of Public Accounts office did the trick.

REAL ESTATE RECORDS

Grantor/Grantee records at the county clerk's office provide documentation on the legal ownership of real property. At the basic level the aim is to search first by both the subject's and the spouse's name. Then second, run any discovered associated names of relatives and close friends to uncover land holdings within your jurisdiction. With increasing computerization of these records, the search becomes an easy routine. Do not omit from your notes the names of attorneys, corporate officers, lending officers, and notaries appearing on the instrument. They may become critical in doing the associative analysis described later in Chapter 11.

How does an investigator find property for a subject in other jurisdictions? The answer involves the use of statewide and nationwide electronic database scans. Our previous discussion mentioned several of these databases:

1. An Officer/Director search (by subject's name) of the Corporate Filings database at your jurisdiction's Secretary of State's office.

2. National Magazine or Newspaper Databases. (NEXIS/LEXIS, DataTimes, National Newspaper Index, Newsbank Electronic Index, Business Periodical Index, ABI/INFORM, Legal Resource Index)

3. OCLC and RLIN. (Available at most major university libraries in the reference area.)

4. CDB Infotek, Information America.

5. Interstate Public Filings. (Available through many information brokers.)

6. Mailing list providers.

7. Disclosure/Spectrum Database, SEC ONLINE.

The investigator running the subject's name on these sources should make note of all localities where the individual has conducted business. Then, the Grantor/Grantee records need checking in each locality to discover possible real estate holdings there.

Additional database scans available through information brokers are:

8. Nationwide Name Search Using Credit Header Information. (This search provides address information from the public portion of a person's credit file. Even though it does not contain the subject's credit history, the Congress and the state legislatures continue to review investigators' right of access. This may be a source denied in the future. Start using the full range of alternatives presented here so you will have tools for tomorrow.)

9. National Mover's Index. (Locates change of address information for subjects.)

10. Name Search of State Motor Vehicle Records. (By running a subject's name, one discovers vehicles owned by him or her in other parts of the state.)

11. Statewide Real Property Searches. (Try Data Research Center at Experian 1-800-421-1052 for membership enrollment. Also, check with your information broker for other resources.)

When an investigator finds a vehicle, boat, aircraft, or public record outside of the subject's current county of residence, the real estate records in the new location must be checked by the person's name. Such a search may produce a summer home, an investment property, or a place of business.

In addition to Grantor/Grantee records, most jurisdictions have a separate tax accessing authority. For example, in Austin, Texas it is called the Travis County Central Appraisal District. The records from this agency can reveal the tax-appraised value of the land and improvements. In some instances, detailed descriptions of the improvements on the property are furnished (the number of rooms, baths, and fixtures). Name searches are possible, and usually phone inquiries are welcome. Checking Appraisal District records can flesh out in dollars the values of the property discovered on the Grantor/Grantee rolls.

PUBLIC RECORD SEARCHING SHORTCUTS

When searching public records, an investigator may save a lot of shoe leather and time by consulting electronic sources first. While these services are not free, they require a subscription or, in the case of Merlin Information Services, buying a CD-ROM, a long journey can become a short one with their use. The key ones to consider are:

1. Dun and Bradstreet (*www.dnb.com*), telephone 800-362-3425. Sign up to access their web site and use their public filings database to locate suits, liens, judgments, UCC filings, and incorporation information

2. CDB Infotek (*www.cdb com*) 800-992-7889 This service has similar business public record searches to Dun and Bradstreet's database. In addition, it has extensive resources on individuals

3. Merlin Information Services (*www.merlindata com*) 800-367-6646. Merlin has online access and CD-ROMs for public records on both individuals and businesses in many jurisdictions in the United States.

SUMMARY

Determine first a subject's occupation, associates, employment, and business holdings. This information is key to understanding the subject's basic financial picture. Use information brokers and university libraries to gain access to national databases such as NEXIS/LEXIS, Interstate Public Filings, CDB Infotek, and Information America to uncover the various records and localities for a subject.

Learn to correlate data from different sources to create an overall picture on the individual. Record the data on the Universal Public Record (Form 13). Summarize the information on the Individual Summary (Form 2). Be sure to check under the subject's name and those of their spouse, associates, and business names in the following sources:

- Real Property Records.
- Motor Vehicle Registration Records.
- Boat Registrations.
- Aircraft Registrations.
- Civil Court Records, including Probate Court.
- Officer/Director Corporate Records.
- UCC Filings.
- Tax Liens.
- Bankruptcy Records.
- Criminal Records.
- Driver's License Records.

Form 2

Individual Summary Form

Case: Client: Subject:

Cross-references to Businesses:

Date Commenced: Date Finished:

DOB: SSN: Spouse:

Addresses:

Banking:

Source   *Date*   *Account Info.*

Vehicles:

Boats:

Form 2

Continued

Aircraft:

Real Estate:

Occupations and Self-Employment:

Earnings:

Driver's License Check:

Criminal Check:

Drive-By Residence:

Form 2

Continued

Probate:

_____

Civil Suits:

_____

Corporations: (Officer/Director)

_____

UCC Filings:

_____

Tax Liens:

_____

Bankruptcy:

_____

Chapter 4

INFORMATION BROKERS
AND OTHER SOURCES

Information brokers, if properly employed, open key avenues. This chapter explains their effective use in asset "detective work." In addition, it will describe sleuthing techniques involving reference works found in major libraries. The reader will learn the various directories for finding the names of organizations and kindred business information.

The information industry rapidly evolves and changes. Look upon the electronic references cited in this work as starting points. Expect name changes of products and repackaging of services to be routine events. Service charges will rise and fall among acquisitions and mergers in the industry.

The crucial focus must remain on how an investigator can continue to exploit the information market. He or she must have enough savvy to perceive alternatives when new obstacles appear. That savvy comes from talking and listening to other investigators. Keep your information networking lines open by attending seminars and sharing your knowledge with others.

INFORMATION BROKERS

An information broker (IB) provides database services to private investigators usually for a per-search service fee. By using such services, investigators save the expense of monthly service charges to a rather large array of database vendors. One does not have to subscribe directly to DIALOG, CDB Infotek, and other providers to take full advantage of them. This saves on overhead, especially if one has a small or medium-sized investigative firm.

What are the best ways to locate information brokers? First, many information brokers are investigators themselves. By attending national and regional investigator meetings, these people will make themselves known by being speakers, by passing out brochures, or by simple socializing. Meetings sponsored by the National Association of Legal Investigators (NALI), the World Association of Detectives, or state investigator organizations like TALI (Texas Association of Licensed Investigators) provide quality contacts.

Another source is to ask other investigators for references on whom they use. The local librarian should have directories of information brokers for reference. Investigative magazines like NALI's *The Legal Investigator* run articles and advertisements by information vendors and brokers. For a detailed explanation of what information brokers can do, reading *The Information Broker's Handbook* by Sue Rugge and Alfred Glossbrenner (McGraw-Hill, 1992) will offer good insight.

Keep in mind though an important factor. An investigator does not have the luxury to dump a vaguely formed inquiry into an information broker's lap like Monday's laundry. Then, upon returning later, expecting a remarkable result, the investigator confronts only disappointment. When asking an IB to do a search, keep it clear, simple, and straightforward. The ideally crafted search uses a name, social security number, address, or date of birth that is the product of careful prior research. Develop a working relationship with several information brokers. Get them to recognize your particular needs in financial investigations. However, make both of your jobs easier by creating searches that are clear and understandable from the start.

IB's have proliferated in the investigative world. Trying to list them all would be beyond the scope of this book. However, for those readers who require some sort of a starting point, what follows is a brief posting:

IRSC, Fullerton, California 800-640-4772
KnowX, *www.knowx.com*
Merlin Information Services, 800-367-6646, *www.merlindata.com*
OPEN, 800-935-OPEN, *www openonline.com*
World Wide Data, 805-634-6380
CDB Infotek, 800-992-7889, *www cdb.com*
North American Information, 888-390-2292
Public Record Links, *www.pac-info.com*
Security Management Online, *www securitymanagement com*

While *Security Management,* a publication of the American Society for Industrial Security (ASIS), is not an IB per se, its web site offers links to numerous investigative and public record sites.

Always check the references of any proprietary IB to make sure they provide good service and adhere to the law in selling information.

Whenever an investigator starts to use an IB, they need to double-check, whenever possible, the IB's work product by other sources. Even when an IB is established, use their work product as the initial starting point and not as the "end game." An IB may offer a search package called an "Asset Check" for a flat fee. It can be repackaged immediately as your work product. Always confirm, whenever feasible, the data provided by such a package. If you cannot corroborate its key data by additional sources, then so state to the client in your report. Remain the investigator, not just the information reseller.

What are the typical services on an IB's menu? A few of IRSC's offerings include:

1. Locator Searches
   - By Social Security Number
   - By Name (Statewide)
   - Vehicle Name Index (an "alpha" search)
2. Business Searches
   - Business Public Filings
   - UCC Index
   - Business Profile (includes a National Business Report)
3. Background/Asset Investigation Searches
   - Bankruptcy Filings
   - Asset Searches
   - Business Credit Report

Please keep in mind that this represents only a small portion of what is available on IRSC and other services. Unfortunately, many investigators restrict themselves to using IB's only to run social security numbers or license plates. The background and advanced asset search features remain greatly underutilized. Upon request, most IB's will gladly provide technical assistance on how to use the complete range of their services. Some IB's, like IRSC, offer regional seminars in effective search strategies. Whatever broker that you use, be sure to become familiar with how to do searches on their system. For each search, know the specific data required to do it effectively. For example, a credit header search needs the full name, SSN, and last known address of the subject to be completely reliable.

Fair Credit Reporting Act (FCRA)

The FCRA places restrictions on accessing an individual's (not a business') credit history. The general rule of thumb is that there must be a legitimate business, connection between the subject and the party desiring access. Some instances where access is permissible include:

1. By permission from the subject.
2. By court order.
3. When the subject is seeking credit with the party.
4. During certain pre-employment investigations.
5. When the subject is applying for insurance with the party.
6. Collection of a judgment.
7. When the party is engaged in a business transaction with the party.

Always obtain proper legal counsel before accessing an individual's credit file. Any legitimate information broker will make you aware of the restrictions under the FCRA. The broker will also require, in most cases, for you to state the lawful reason under which you seek access before granting the same to you. (Information brokers usually provide additional background knowledge concerning the state credit and privacy laws of their jurisdiction. Consult with them on these issues as the need arises.)

OTHER DATABASE PROVIDERS

NEXIS and LEXIS are services of Mead Data Central in Dayton, Ohio (800-346-9759). While setting up individual accounts is possible, the cost of these services usually restricts their availability to universities, large public libraries, newspapers, and broadcasting companies. Check with your local library to see if their contract permits searches for the public. For example, the State Law Library in Austin does NEXIS/LEXIS for the public at cost. Otherwise, your affiliation with a university or a local newspaper may permit access. NEXIS contains libraries of news information compiled from major newspapers, periodicals, and news program transcripts from around the country. When searching on NEXIS, one specifies a library such as General

News, a file such as Current (last 2-3 years), and a unique source such as *The New York Times*. Searches take the form of single terms, key-words, truncated terms (report** = reported, reporter, reports), seg-ments (company [Honda]), and by dates. The service also offers com-bined Current File searches which enables an investigator to scan many news sources for a particular time frame.

LEXIS has libraries on Patents, Copyrights, and Trademarks, the Code of Federal Regulations, Federal Taxation, Federal Law, and States' Law. The service also provides access to Securities and Exchange Commission (SEC) filings (10-Ks and 10-Qs, reports required of public corporations annually and quarterly). The search methodologies are similar to those of NEXIS. NEXIS/LEXIS is a powerful scanning tool to see if your subject appears in newspapers of record. It enables reporters to develop quick background information on persons and business that suddenly come into news prominence. For investigators, it may seem like having their own private intelli-gence gathering service.

InfoTrac, Business Periodicals Index (BPI), Legal Resource Index (LRI), and National Newspaper Index (NNI) are magazine and news-paper indexes from Information Access Company in Foster City, California. InfoTrac and NNI offer references on articles of general interest. BPI and LRI specialize in business and legal subjects, respec-tively. Searches consist of entering a key word or phrase which pro-duces a list of articles containing the search term. These databases are found in large public libraries and at university libraries on either CD-ROM or at an on-line terminal. They offer a solid alternative or adjunct to NEXIS/LEXIS for doing background scans.

ABI/INFORM is a large database compiled from leading business magazines. For picking up background facts on established public and private companies, it can be an excellent source. One can search by abstract content, company name, geographic location, key word descriptions, and by Standard Industrial Classification Codes (SIC). The database is available through DIALOG, Knowledge Index, and on CD-ROM at university libraries.

For locating corporate officer information and ownership data on public companies, SEC ONLINE is a good source to go to when you suspect an individual may have large business interests.

DIALOG is a gateway to a huge family of technical, business, and academic databases. Located in Palo Alto, California (800-334-2564), it provides access to the Disclosure/Spectrum database of SEC filings.

It also has several business databases which can be helpful in business credit and background inquiries (more about this later). Since DIA-LOG is a rather complex service to use, a novice's best bet is to obtain a reference librarian's assistance at first. Many public libraries offer searches on DIALOG done at cost by the reference staff. If one desires later to do their own searches, training is available through DIALOG's classes held around the nation.

An investigator should not overlook consumer-oriented databases such as CompuServe and America Online. Subscriptions to these services are available in most software stores. CompuServe has a service called I-Quest which brings hundreds of commercially produced databases to your office or home computer. Many of the electronic information sources previously discussed are on I-Quest. In addition, CompuServe has Special Interest Groups (SIGs) on subjects as diverse as astronomy, law, business, medicine, ham radio, and so on. If you need to find an expert quickly, checking the SIGs will provide a shortcut.

For example, the person who knows the capitalization requirements for a small software publishing company (maybe just like the one you are investigating) could be a member of the software industry SIG. I once researched a nursing home's finances by placing a generic notice on the bulletin board for the medical SIG. I received several electronic mail (E-MAIL) messages in response, which greatly aided my investigation. They identified what public documents were available for reviewing the home's Medicare and other governmental income.

America Online (AOL) also has an extensive number of SIGs which can be a source of information and experts. In addition, AOL offers keyword database searching of major newspapers like *The Chicago Tribune* and periodicals such as *PC World*. In one case, I located the history of a small software manufacturer from a newspaper article in a San Francisco area paper on the AOL service. All it took was running the name on the paper's back issues database. In addition, information age services like *Wired*, a "hip" magazine about electronic community issues like computer privacy, and Cyberlex, a column about computers and the law, make AOL a powerful information navigator. Scanning the business news services for information on a targeted company is easy on AOL. A simple keyword search does it. Also, company profiles of major corporations are available through the Business Center on AOL.

BUSINESS SOURCES

For quick reference on small and "fly-by-night" businesses, touching base with the local Better Business Bureau may yield useful background. Also, look to see if the business is in the local yellow pages. The advertisement there may answer many of the fundamental questions:

- What type of legal structure does the business have?
- When was it formed?
- Who are the principal owners or officers?
- What are its principal product lines or services?
- How many people does it employ?
- What are its annual sales?

Check the local newspaper for other advertisements by the business. Read the employment classifieds to learn if they are hiring. Make note of what types of jobs they have open and the extent of the compensation packages. Often, employment classifieds go far in providing basic data about a business.

The local business newspaper may have an editor or reporter who could supply answers to the fundamental questions. Contacting the business editor of the city newspaper may also be helpful. A call to the chamber of commerce could yield publications profiling the general business climate in the area. The target business may have ads or articles in the publication. In addition, the chamber may publish profiles of certain local industries, supplying overall statistical information, with a possible spotlight on the target firm.

Do not overlook the business information center at your local public library. They may have a collection of directories of local businesses which provide biographical and statistical information. Also, they could have statewide directories of businesses. For example, the Austin Public Library has the *Directory of Texas Manufacturers* (published annually) which supplies answers to most of the fundamental search questions concerning manufacturers in the state.

The same library also has national directories such as Dun and Bradstreet's *Million Dollar Directory* and the *Thomas Register of Manufacturers*. If you suspect the local business is a major concern, checking these directories could be profitable. The Dun's Business

Identification Service microfiche briefly describes over ten million companies listed with them, and it may also be available at your public library. I have used the one at the Austin library many times to find multiple business locations for a target. Additionally, one may wish to search Dun's Electronic Business Directory through DIALOG. It has basic address information on over eight million companies. Also on DIALOG one finds Dun's Market Identifiers, Dun's Financial Records Plus, and electronic versions of the *Million Dollar Directory* and the *Thomas Register*. Dun's Market Identifiers has basic information on over two million businesses. Dun's Financial Records Plus has financial statements on over 650,000 businesses.

Whenever an investigator needs to learn how to access a directory for a given business field, they need to ask the reference librarian for *Directories in Print* by Gale Research. If, for example, a commercially published directory for condom manufacturers exists, this book will tell you how to obtain it. If you do not wish to purchase the listed directory, your librarian may obtain a copy for you through inter-library loan.

Nationwide newspaper databases such as NEXIS, DataTimes (800-642-2525), and National Newspaper Index should be used if the target business operates outside of your locality. Also, databases such as Interstate Public Filings, Business Public Filings, CDB Infotek, and Information America need scanning when possible national business interests become a factor. Of course, for publicly owned companies, an investigator can use the Disclosure/Spectrum database through DIALOG. LEXIS can also provide access to Securities and Exchange Commission (SEC) filings.

Other database searches on DIALOG that may be helpful include:

1. Standard & Poor's Register–Biographical. (Lists the directors and executives of firms with over $1 million in sales.)

2. Company Intelligence. (Compiled from over three thousand periodicals, this service indexes news about companies with gross annual sales over $500,000.)

3. Corporate Affiliations. (Who owns what? A corporate family tree.)

An investigator should not overlook what business information is on CD-ROM. Reference books which have extensive listings include:

1. The *Encyclopedia of Business Information Sources* by Gale Research (1988) contains listings by topic of many reference works in print and

on CD-ROM of interest to investigators.

2. *CD-ROMs in Print* by Meckler in Westport, CT publishes an annual (since 1987) description of information available in this format.

3. *Magazines for Libraries,* 7th edition, 1992, by Bill and Linda S. Katz, published by R.R. Bowker, lists virtually every magazine: general, technical, and scholarly that a library may wish to stock. The books describe the various formats, including CD-ROM, that each magazine has available.

4. Dennis King's *Get the Facts on Anyone* (Prentice-Hall, 1992) identifies several CD-ROM sources that he uses regularly as an investigative reporter.

5. *Directories in Print,* 1993, by Gale Research, lists any commercial directories in print, microform, and in CD-ROM formats.

Your local reference librarian should be helpful in locating these books. One must not forget trade or professional organizations existing both locally and nationally. Check the local newspaper in the business section for a weekly listing of local business and trade meetings. The newspaper staff should be able to supply the names of contact persons for the relevant organization. In contacting these individuals, state that you are doing a research paper on this local business and need some background information. National and international trade organizations are available by consulting:

1. *Directory of European Associations.*
2. *Encyclopedia of Associations.*
3. *World Guide to Trade Associations.*
4. *National Trade and Professional Associations of the United States and Canada and Labor Unions.*
5. *Encyclopedia of Associations, International.*

They should be all well-known to the public library's reference desk.

Experian business credit reports are available on the information service CompuServe for about thirteen million businesses. IB's who belong to Dun and Bradstreet can offer access to credit reports on over nine million businesses. Of course, supplier and vendor interviews, UCC filings, Business Public Filings, national and local business press coverage, and general business reference works like the *Million Dollar Directory* can contribute to the creditworthiness picture.

Non-profit organizations listed on the Internal Revenue Service's *Cumulative List of Organizations* must file a financial disclosure form 990 with the IRS. The organization must make available for public inspection at their offices the last three years of its form 990 filings. Usually, the organization will provide a copy by mail. Private foundations must file a form 990-PF which is also public (see Chap. 8).

NEWSGROUPS

Newsgroups act like bulletin boards where users or members may post messages exchanging comments and ideas or seeking information on a given topic. One of the best ways to search for information contained within news groups is to use *www.deja.com* also known as *www.dejanews.com.* Using keyword searches, an investigator can find information or persons-in-the-know on almost any topic. in addition, many web search engines now provide the option of searching newsgroups too.

Newsgroups are the bulletin boards (or gossip boards) of the Internet. They contain huge amounts of information on subjects ranging from collectibles to the details of incorporating in Zaire. Organized by topics, commonly called hierarchies, an investigator would find the following general classifications:

comp-	Dealing with computers.
misc-	Miscellaneous topics.
news-	Internet news.
rec-	Hobbies and recreation.
sci-	Science.
soc-	Social groups.
talk-	Debates, usually on politics.
alt-	Alternative groups. Many investigative topics are found here.
comp.virus-	Computers viruses.
talk.politics.crypto-	Cryptography.
misc.invest.stocks-	Stocks and options.

Obviously, some of these newsgroups pertaining to assets like boats, cars, stocks, and collectibles have direct value to the financial investigator. Do not forget about them as a resource when doing financial investigations (see also Chapter 13).

Examples of various newsgroups include:

rec.autos.marketplace-	Values of automobiles.

rec.arts.tv-	Discussions of television.
rec.collecting-	Collectibles.
misc.legal.computing-	The Law and Computers.

BIOGRAPHICAL SOURCES

In addition to running a subject's name through the several periodical databases, an investigator should not overlook Gale Research's *Biography and Genealogy Master Index*. This reference work, available at major libraries, may lead you to the names of relatives, even if the target is not cited personally. Consult Marquis' *Who's Who* series (*Index to Marquis Who's Who Publications, Who's Who in America*, etc.) when doing background investigations on prominent individuals. Other reference works include:

1. H. W. Wilson Company's *Biography Index*.
2. Robert B. Slocum's *Biographical Dictionaries and Related Works*.
3. *Directory of Medical Specialists*.
4. *Martindale-Hubbell Law Directory*.
5. [ABMS] *American Board of Medical Specialties' Compendium of Certified Medical Specialists*.
6. *Directory of American Scholars*.

Research Centers

If you are doing background on an individual or business involved in an unusual product line or service, locating a library with a research collection in that subject area can be essential. The *Directory of Special Libraries and Information Centers* fills that need. It describes the location and the nature of the holdings of each specialty library. With an explanation of the library's services to the public, it is an invaluable resource to an investigator. Need a library on computer crime or the coffee industry? You will find them here.

Additionally, *Directories in Print, Newsletters in Print,* and *Standard Periodical Directory* can lead to information resources on arcane subjects. *Research Centers Directory* and *New Research Centers* provide access to repositories of unusual data. Use your imagination in background investigation. The library collection or expert on your subject or your subject's business may only be one phone call away.

Table 2
USEFUL RESEARCH SOURCES

Source	Applications
1. *Encyclopedia of Associations.*	Locate almost any professional group.
2. Dun's Business identification.	Where a business operates.
3. *Directories in Print.*	The key to business and trade directories.
4. *Newsletters in Print.*	Identifies industry newsletters.
5. *Million Dollar Directory.*	Short profiles on public and private companies. (In print, CD-ROM, and online formats.)
6. *Directory of Special Libraries*	A guide to special research collections.
7. Experian, Dun and Bradstreet.	Business credit sources. (Online access.)
8. *InfoTrac:* Legal Resource, Business Periodical index	National periodical databases. (CD-ROM.)
9. *Thomas Register of Manufacturers.*	Useful for locating suppliers and vendors.

Chapter 5

VISITING THE SUBJECT'S PREMISES

The home, neighborhood, and neighbors of a subject will tell a tale about that person's finances. Learning how "to read" the subject's premises forms the basis of this brief chapter. Every house has its own unique story. The story starts at the local tax appraisal district office. There, an investigator researches the evaluations of the land and buildings. One discovers the age of the house and a detailed listing of the number and type of rooms. Previous years' evaluations show additions or improvements over time, a key to gauging rising prosperity. This data gives the investigator some rough dollar values on the residence. In addition, one learns whether the dwelling is a qualified homestead. (A homestead may be exempt from collection action in your jurisdiction.) And, checking if the subject owns non-exempt land elsewhere in the county is no problem.

DRIVE-BY OF RESIDENCE

A quick snapshot of the subject's residence while driving by does not constitute proper fact gathering. Careful observation is in order. Without violating privacy laws, use some sort of cover (meter reader or delivery person) to get close to the property. Make note of any vehicles, recreational equipment such as all-terrain vehicles or jet skis, boats, travel trailers, or mobile homes. If you can act unimpeded, be sure to record all registration and license plate numbers.

Are there any signs of a business being operated from the premises? For example, do the vehicles have business trade names painted on their sides? Does the garage look like a machine shop or woodworking mill? Are there signs on the property such as "Art's Bookkeeping Service" or "Acme Computer Consultants"? If you see these types of signs, checking with the state sales tax or corporate records agency will give you more detailed information on the business. If the home has more than one electrical meter, one may serve the residence and the other the business. The local electric utility may supply details about billing and power usage.

In addition to occupational information, look for other clues such as a realtor's FOR SALE sign or a contractor's advertisement. Calling the realtor later, posing as a potential buyer, may reveal valuable information about the seller. A contractor could tell you that he just installed a new swimming pool or added a room to the house.

Does the home have an alarm system? There may be a good reason for the owner making that investment. A coin, art, or historical collection needs protecting. Checking at the local police department will uncover any reports of burglaries for the location. Previous reports may establish the existence of a special collection. The crime analysis bureau at the police department could supply the crime statistics for that neighborhood. If the subject has extensive anti-theft defenses in place in a low crime area, it could indicate nervous concern about a collection or valuables stored in the home. Further investigation about the subject's hobbies and interests may be in order.

Note how the house and grounds appear. Good upkeep is a sign of financial stability. Also, note the general appearance of the neighborhood. Is it a quiet, comfortable neighborhood with well-kept homes and lawns? Or, does an open-air drug mart operate a few yards away? Place as much objective description in your report as possible. You may wish to check the economic rating of the area later in a Cole's crisscross directory. This directory breaks down geographical areas into census tracts. It rates each tract on an economic scale from the poorest to the wealthiest. Adding this data to your report adds an element of authority in evaluating the neighborhood.

Do not overlook the front door for various notices. In one investigation, I found the electric department's notice of service shutoff and a civil lawsuit citation both tacked to the subject's front door. After writing down the lawsuit's case number, I was able to research it at the courthouse and then contact the plaintiff's attorney. I learned from the attorney that the subject was a scofflaw with the habit of running up debts in a city and then splitting town for a friendlier place. The attorney had to get special service ordered on the individual since this defendant remained a constant moving target.

By keeping one's eyes open, an investigator can learn much. Driving by on trash day, one may see boxes for recently purchased computers or appliances. A tall tower by the house may reveal the subject is a HAM radio or TV operator. A call to the local HAM or computer club chapter may reveal the investment the subject has in his or her hobby. Old cars and engine parts in the backyard may be signs of an auto rebuilding or a racing car business.

Surveillance

Try to be at the residence when everyone leaves for work or school. Note the children's clothing. Is it the latest fashion or hand-me-downs? How are the parents dressed? Are they in suits or fast-food server uniforms? As Arthur Conan Doyle counseled in the Sherlock Holmes stories, an investigator can learn a great deal about people from their dress and demeanor. Keep your eyes open for these details. If the family car stays in the garage at night, the morning surveillance will reveal its make, model, year, and license plate number. The type of vehicle may be a good indicator of economic status.

Do not rule out doing a moving surveillance of the family vehicle as the morning rounds occur. Are the children dropped off at a private school? Where do the parents work? Before work, do the parents work out at an exclusive health club or breakfast in an expensive restaurant? In big cases, consider daylong surveillance over a period of a week. The observant investigator may discover a debtor that pleads the poorhouse before creditors but actually lives a lavish life-style.

Follow your imagination, and the so-called drive-by can be very productive for your client.

A WORD ABOUT TRASH

When an investigator needs a telephone bill, a bank statement, invoices, and other financial records, heading for the trash may do the trick. The key is not to violate the law while doing this investigative technique. Be sure of the legal requirements in your jurisdiction before undertaking this activity.

Trash produces more than the explicit financial document for the investigator. It may contain the airline ticket to the Cayman Islands or the telephone bill showing the call to a bank there. Trash also acts as a covert channel for information. An increase in a certain type of waste or trash may signal a change in a business's operations or product lines. A sharp increase or decline in the amount of scrap could indicate serious internal problems in a business. At the consumer level, a sudden increase or decrease in the types of throwaways found could signal financial prosperity or hardship. Learn to read the trash for more than just financial documents.

Reading the Trash

The investigator should strive to be an archaeologist of sorts. These scientists recreate how people lived through the artifacts (trash) that they left behind. The same principle works for latter-day households. By considering how the well-to-do family lives, the investigator establishes a model for what their trash should contain. For example, the lack of packages in the trash for convenience foods may indicate a tight budget. With time at a premium nowadays, people will spend money on frozen convenience foods and meals, if they can afford it.

If people have the money, they will purchase premium foods such as steak, specially prepared poultry, and fish. Home delivery items such as pizza, oriental food, and fast-food sandwiches will probably be present. The residue packaging will be evident.

Personal care products and cosmetics will be prominent in a household with surplus income. They could be scarce in one just getting by.

The lack of newspapers, bottles, and aluminum cans in the home's recycling bin could indicate a reduction in consumer purchases. The more a household recycles, the more people or consumption that it has. High levels of consumption are indicators of possible prosperity. The question becomes: "How are they paying for it?"

If the financial documents in the trash indicate payment by cash (sales receipts) or by checks (bank statements), then the income probably matches or exceeds the expenditures. However, if credit card slips or statements predominate as the method of payment, the household may operate beyond its means. Correlating the non-financial materials with the financial records in the trash may reveal a household's cash flow situation.

One should not overlook who brings out the trash. Is it a family member? Or, could it be a domestic servant? Households with large disposable incomes employ domestic workers, not those in dire financial straits.

Items of conspicuous consumption in the trash divulge much about a household's finances. Empty bottles for champagne or fine wines and containers for luxury foods found on a regular basis reveal lavish spending. Receipts for regular weekend travel in distant cities indicate a large disposable income. Subscriptions to luxury catalogues and magazines may be a sign of expensive tastes. Packaging materials for expensive clothes and jewelry are possible clues. Invoices from private clubs, membership papers from spas or exclusive health clubs, or receipts from "gold" and other premium credit cards all may indicate an above average income and life-style.

Regular mail solicitations from stockbrokers, investment bankers, financial planners, and luxury car dealers suggest a well-to-do subject. Brochures, receipts, or confirmations about foreign travel on a regular basis could indicate extensive income. Receipts or packaging materials for luxury electronic goods like big-screen TV's, extensive stereo systems, and elaborate video cameras reveal big dollar spending.

NEIGHBORS

Neighbors may tell you about conspicuous consumption by the subject. Finding their names and telephone numbers is simple when using a crisscross directory. Whether the contact is by phone or in person, keep the approach conversational and even folksy. You may be talking to a treasure chest of leads. An investigator could learn about the boat kept at a nearby lake. Information regarding the weekend home in the mountains is always interesting. That the subject has an airplane at the regional general aviation facility adds spice to the investigation. Hunting adventures from the subject's game lease in another part of the state make for good listening. The news of the recent inheritance by the subject thrills you too.

SUMMARY

Read the residence like a book. Use the tax appraisal records as a preface to gain basic financial and legal information about the site. Eyeballing the place fills in the middle chapters. In looking for vehicles, recreational equipment, and boats, the story slowly builds. Are there signs of business activity at the home? Does the trash reveal any indicators of lavish living or considerable outside income? The final chapters involve contact with the neighbors to tie up the loose ends. They may point you to the "smoking gun" asset that, up until now, remained secret. Friendly conversation here will carry an investigator far. Use Form 3 to record data gathered at the subject's residence.

Form 3

Residence Check

Case: Date:

Subject:

Tax Appraisal District:

    Land Evaluation: Improvements Evaluation:

    Age of Building: Number and Types of Rooms:

    Homestead?   Previous Evaluations:

    Other Properties?

Residence:

    Address: Area Economic Rating?

    Recreational Vehicles or Boats?

    Motor Vehicles?

    Indications of Business Activity?

    Photos taken of house, grounds, and outbuildings?

    Estimates on Square Footage of Buildings:

Form 3

Continued

Utility Usage at Site:

Alarm System in Place?   Type?
                                Company?

Police Report Activity for Location:

General Condition of Grounds?

General Condition of Neighborhood?

Unusual Signs or Notices at Site?

Evidence of Hobbies?

Fixed Surveillance Results: Date: Time of Day:

Additional Fixed Surveillance:

Dates: Time of Day: Results:

Moving Surveillance:

Dates: Time of Day: Results:

Form 3

Continued

Trash: Schedule:

Our Pickup Dates:

Analysis:
Financial Documents Found:

    1. Credit Card Statements and Records:

    2. Bills:

    3. Bank Statements and Cancelled Checks:

    4. Statements from Other Financial Institutions:

    5. Telephone Records:

    6. Travel Records and Receipts:

Other Evidence:

    1. Luxury Consumables:

    2. Luxury Lifestyle:
    (Clothing, jewelry, entertainment receipts, club memberships)

    3. Luxury Purchases:

Form 3

Continued

Interviews with Neighbors:

Dates: How?   Name:

Offsite Lifestyle Activities?

Offsite Properties or Assets?

On-site Lifestyle Activities?

Recent Financial Changes?

Chapter 6

ADVANCED SOURCES FOR INDIVIDUALS

A dvanced methods seek added dimensions to the subject's financial picture. In this chapter, the investigator will consider special issues like agency and third-party liability that accidents bring to financial investigations. One will learn methods for calculating wage earnings. Also, by digging deep into governmental sources like regulatory agencies, an investigator can get "inside" data on an individual. A second look at real estate records will offer new perspectives on a subject's hidden ties to others. The discussion continues with tips on examining financial statements; then, it suggests ideas about investigating unreported income. Finally, the text explains lawsuit abuses to manipulate balance sheets or to deceive creditors.

HOW THE BASIC SEARCH DIFFERS

Do the basic search when a client requests a preliminary or a cursory look at a defendant's financial standing. The intent is not to discover "hidden assets" or to calculate net worth but, rather, the investigator seeks a simple overview. Many financial investigations of individual defendants will terminate upon completing the basic search. The reasons for this abrupt end are several. The plaintiff's lawyer may have a policy limit tender on the table by the defendant's liability carrier. An asset investigation report will demonstrate the attorney acted reasonably before advising that his client sign a release. Or, after the preliminary search, the investigator will determine the subject is obviously judgment-proof. If the defendant is unemployed, has only a 1968 Chevrolet Caprice, and lives in public housing, the case needs closing.

A basic search may yield executable assets, but the attorney decides to investigate the remaining details personally. Or, in doing a complete preliminary search, the investigator documents that the subject has typical middle-class assets. However, after taking into account exemptions against executions, nothing valuable remains. The basic search frequently becomes a "dead-end street."

SPECIAL ISSUES IN ACCIDENT CASES

Yet, the investigator must not become jaded by the percentages. The same common sense that dictates many people are judgment-proof also says that several factors usually cause an accident. Before beginning the advanced search, review the facts of the incident in a brainstorming session.

Ask yourself if agency could be a factor. Was the target acting on behalf of another at the time of the accident? Under the law of agency the other party may be liable for the damages too. Has anyone interviewed the defendant about being on a mission for someone else? Could a third party be liable? Does product liability enter in? Was drinking involved? Could there be a dramshop (a place that sells alcoholic beverages) case lurking somewhere in the record? By reviewing these issues first, whole new possibilities could reveal themselves. Rather than do a perfunctory "asset check," the investigator can start researching a "deep pocket" early in the case. You will win the client's praises if you spot these possibilities and develop them promptly.

WAGE EARNINGS INFORMATION

Once the investigator establishes the subject's occupation (see Chap. 3), several techniques exist for uncovering earnings. First, if the subject is a public-sector employee, then that salary probably is a public record. Checking with the employing department or agency will supply the necessary data. If the subject works in private industry, a call to the personnel department, inquiring after the job category the subject holds, may produce a salary range for that type of job.

The U.S. Department of Labor publishes *Area Wage Survey* for many metropolitan areas on a periodic basis. These surveys are available at most public libraries. For example, the 1990 survey for Austin lists many common occupations, such as the following two:

| Motor Vehicle Mechanics | $11.85/hr. (average) |
| Computer Systems Analysts | $730 to $983 weekly (middle range) |

The agency also publishes *Employment and Earning* on a monthly basis for nationwide data. *American Salaries and Wages* by Arsen Darnay (Gale Research, Inc., 1991), available in public libraries, gives the low, middle, and high salaries for most occupations by locales.

Finally, the extrapolation of earnings from known assets can be a useful technique. Suppose the investigator determines a subject owns two vehicles: a 1991 Ford Taurus and a 1991 Mercury Topaz. Using N.A.D.A. guides on car values (available at the public library), the investigator establishes their retail value. He then contacts a bank loan officer to determine the earnings level needed to qualify for the loan required to purchase the vehicles. Other assets such as boats, real estate, and aircraft could form the basis for similar estimates. The investigator obtains values by contacting dealers, agents, and brokers.

An ideal arrangement would be to create a financial statement based upon the research of the subject's assets and liabilities. Then, the investigator could call a bank loan officer as a prospective borrower. If asked about his earnings, the investigator can quote a figure, and then mention that he could bring in co-signers if needed. The feedback from the loan officer should provide the necessary income bracket data. Then, the investigator would place any wage or income estimate information on the Individual Summary (Form 2).

GOVERNMENTAL SOURCES

Always investigate whether a target requires a license to conduct a business or profession. For example, if someone operates an air-conditioning repair service, they need a state or local license in most jurisdictions. In Texas, that license requires a policy of liability insurance. In doing a basic asset search, I learned the owner of the defendant's vehicle had a six-figure umbrella liability policy on file with the state regulatory agency for air-conditioning contractors. This discovery converted the case from one where the client had to settle for minimum limits to one where extended compensation was possible.

Licensing agencies provide excellent background material on subjects. Applications, letters of reference, test results, complaints on file, and other documents can identify associates and relatives. Certain licensed professions and businesses require limited credit and financial information as a part of the application. For example, to start a proprietary school in Texas, the state requires a financial statement prepared by an accountant to be a part of the application.

Regulatory agencies may have extensive files regarding a specific business. These files usually contain hearing transcripts and investigative reports. For example, if an investigator needed to research a Texas trucking company, they could check the records of the Texas Railroad Commission. Or, like in a case I researched against a hospital, I found detailed financial information in the hearings before the Texas Department of Health. Officers of businesses may speak frankly about financial matters in order to win governmental approval of a project. Check over indexes carefully at the regulatory agency involved with your target. You may uncover a gold mine of information concerning finances and associates. Do not overlook testimony at the local level: before the zoning board or the city council. Checking the indexes to the minutes at your city clerk's office may be worthwhile.

Vast amounts of information exist on businesses at the state and federal level. Use your state's Governmental Manual to locate agencies that do extensive contracting with the private sector. The open records laws in your jurisdiction may allow access to contract documents. The Freedom of Information Act request, if properly crafted, will provide contract information at the federal level. Two excellent guides to getting all kinds of information from the federal government are Matthew Lesko's *Info-Power and Information U.S.A.,* available at most bookstores. *Info-Power* is also available on CD-ROM, allowing keyword searches.

If an individual holds public office, limited financial data may be on file at the city clerk's office, Secretary of State, or at the Federal Election Commission. I researched a Texas politician's campaign filings with relative ease at the Secretary of State's office. They were well organized and indexed; the staff was most helpful. The filings proved a fund of information about associates, friends, and contributors.

REAL ESTATE RECORDS (A SECOND LOOK)

The initial examination of these records in Chapter 3 served to identify the *extent* of property holdings. A second look at the records involves searching for financial and power connections between the documents' principals and ancillary names appearing within. Make a list of the attorneys, notaries, co-signers, witnesses, and bank or mortgage officers from the records. Do names reappear? Do they sound familiar? Where *else* do they surface in the public record on the case? A good investigator asks these questions; they lead to new understandings. In complex cases, the use of an index card system or a computer database will aid in tracking names (see Chap. 11).

Another financial maneuver to watch is using real estate to launder illegal funds or to hide undisclosed income. An individual may have disposable income from investments in other jurisdictions. Real estate provides a good place to stash it away. When a person's land holdings appear to exceed what their disclosed earnings can support, take a second look:

1. From the subject's credit report or financial statement, list all her debts.
2. Total the subject's assets from the Individual Summary (Form 2).
3. Calculate the subject's income based upon her occupation (see the previous "Wage Earnings" section).
4. Subtract the debts from the assets to give a rough net worth. If the net worth exceeds greatly her annual income multiplied by five years, then consider checking into sources of unreported income (see next two sections).

FINANCIAL STATEMENTS

Investigating real estate could lead you to financial statements filed with lenders. If a subject defaulted on a mortgage, the lender could be trying to collect the outstanding balance. They may be willing to share information. In reviewing an individual's financial statement, first look for the overstating of assets.

The borrower may list stocks or securities which are not publicly traded. The bonds listed may not be rated. Claiming ownership interests, which are difficult to confirm, in private companies or limited partnerships is possible. In other words, the potential borrower blowing a smoke screen of dubious assets, in order to get a loan, happens more often than you think. This book emphasizes uncovering valid assets. However, the investigator must keep in mind that financial investigation includes discovering bogus assets and liabilities. Touting to a client that the subject has all these wonderful assets, when in fact they turn out to be virtually worthless or non-existent, will not win the investigator any friends. Sometimes "deadbeats" really are judgment-proof. Carefully investigating the validity of any assets or liabilities will prevent the perpetuating of illusions.

In any major investigation, seek the expert help of a NASD (National Association of Securities Dealers) securities dealer to review any financial statements from the subject. The same goes for any securities portfolio. A qualified NASD dealer can research the actual market values. Comparisons with the values declared in the financial statement will reveal how generous the subject was in inflating his portfolio. Keep in mind that securities do change in value over time. If the financial statement is a couple of years old, checking past values at that time is no problem. The public library will have several reference works like past issues of *The New York Times* or *The Wall Street Journal* on microform and *Value Line* (for the past year) to supply the necessary figures.

Evaluating limited partnerships and other similar investment vehicles may require the assistance of a securities dealer and an accountant. As we will discuss in the next chapter, the more exotic investment plans are good places to hide assets. They also provide opportunities to make others think that the subject has more wealth than he or she really possesses. Do not be afraid to get expert assistance in examining these complex investment tools.

Unreported Income

Sources of unreported income include proceeds from otherwise legitimate investments and from illegal earnings. Legitimate investments take the form of stock dividends, payments from annuities, royalties, and rent payments. These investments may be in other names, from out-of-state institutions, or held in a business name. In any event, the aim is to have them remain unknown to creditors and tax collectors. Two common methods for uncovering their existence are trash surveillance (see Chap. 5) and the analysis of bank statements or financial statements.

Illegal earnings originate from "working under the table," criminal activities, or hidden ownership of a business. Surveillance can unmask secret employment or moonlighting. Common criminal activities include illegal gaming and drug distribution. Surveillance will work here too. In addition, checking local newspaper indexes, courthouse criminal files, and the local police database will bring past convictions and arrests to light. The scanning techniques presented in Chapters 1-3 should help uncover a subject's hidden ownership of a business. UCC filings and Officer/Director scans may trip the subject's hand. Chapters 7, 8, and 12 also deal with techniques on piercing the veil of hidden ownership.

Once an investigator establishes that an unreported income source exists, its impact upon the subject's overall cash flow is not difficult to measure. Using a method known as "Source and Application," the investigator first gathers the subject's living expenses. These figures include: household expenses, insurance, auto repair costs, mortgage payments, vehicle payments, taxes, medical expenses, and entertainment costs.

If exact figures are lacking, one can develop reliable estimates using the subject's real and private property holdings as a base. For example, if the year, make, and model of the car is known, by using the N.A.D.A. guides for car values and a loan table (available from banks), an investigator can estimate monthly payments. Similar calculations apply to mortgage, boat payments, and so on. An investigator may wish to use a loan table program on a personal computer. They are available with many home finance programs for PC's. A local public librarian can help in locating statistical data from the federal government or private sources on average living expenses, broken down by category, for various size households. (Try *Statistics Sources,* 13th Edition, 1990 and *Statistical Abstract of the United States,* 1992.) If the utility consumption is known, calculating monthly bills would be straightforward.

Add together all of the expenses. Then, subtract the amount of the *known* income gathered by research described earlier in the chapter. The resulting difference is the amount of income from unknown or illegal sources. If the difference is significant, the investigator will need to have his client subpoena all income and expense records. The investigation will move from estimation techniques to proving the actual figures. Once the hard numbers get admitted into evidence, pinning down the subject on this issue may force a settlement.

LAWSUITS (ANOTHER LOOK)

Also, a second look at the lawsuits involving the targets may yield repeating lists of names or types of lawsuits. Asking why a company files so many contract or collection actions may lead to new insight. Is this much litigation common for this line of business? Or, does this activity signify manipulating of balance sheets through sweetheart lawsuits? Could one of the involved companies be a shell, acting as a magnet for bad debts while the other businesses operate debt-free?

Researching the background players such as the lawyers or witnesses may reveal the subtext of what is going on. Personal injury lawsuits against principal targets that settle quickly deserve close scrutiny. What were they trying to keep from the public? Those that sue your target could be enemies with an axe to grind. They may tell you enough about your target to fill many investigative notebooks.

FINANCIAL INVESTIGATIONS:
A TOOL FOR SECURITY MANAGERS

An astute investigator does not limit the locating and evaluating of assets to just those who owe his client money. Often, with persons in positions of trust, doing a routine check on their finances serves to reassure that trust. Financial background investigations detect conflicts of interest, an officer owning or consulting with a business in competition, possible outright embezzlements, and unauthorized appropriations of company funds or resources for personal use. In addition, financial surveillance may uncover an executive who is spying for a competitor.

The ruling principle must be "never let things go too far." Regular, routine investigations of employees in sensitive positions often identify problems before they get out of hand. All key executives and employees in sensitive financial or technological positions need to sign an authorization, upon hire, for routine background checks during their employment. Defining which positions are sensitive will vary from company to company. The rule of thumb, however, should be that any employee whose breach of trust could cause grave harm to the company must receive the "sensitive label." Grave harm means impacting the company's bottom line by five (5) percentage points or better.

Security must refrain from creating a totalitarian or "Big Brother" atmosphere. All routine background investigations must remain low-key, unobtrusive, and non-adversarial, whenever possible. Only when significant information develops in the routine check that something is awry should more intensive investigation activities begin (see Chapters 6 and 7 for more on in-depth investigations). So, routine background investigations should include:

1. A public records scan using a service like Merlin information Services or CDB Infotek under the subject's name. Make note of any business owned by the subject or where he or she serves as an officer or director (see Chapter 13).
2. Checking the names of all directors and officers of any known businesses owned by the subject. (This information is available through Dun and Bradstreet or the Secretary of State's office.)
3. If not done in item 1, run UCC (Uniform Commercial Code) filings on the subject and his or her businesses in the subject's state of residence and in every state where you locate a known business (again, Merlin or CDB Infotek can help here).
4. Run the subject's name and the names of any businesses involving the subject on several search engines for the Internet. Do not forget to check newsgroups also (see Chapters 4 and 13).
5. Do a criminal record search in the jurisdiction where the subject lives from the present back five years. Supplement this check with running the subject's name on the CO-ROM database for the local newspaper in the jurisdiction for the last years. If the subject spends significant amounts of time in another jurisdiction each year, run the same checks there too.
6. Do a routine audit of the company's accounts for the subject. Obviously, the company's audit staff can assist here. This should be a scan of transactions, not a detailed examination of every expense. Look for transactions that are out of place. For

example, a trip to Los Angeles including a side trip to Las Vegas or to Tijuana may require scrutiny. Or, relatively large expenses labeled "entertainment" or "general merchandise" without further itemization or explanation may require careful study.

The emphasis should be on scanning the available record, preferably in electronic form whenever possible. One looks for anomalies in the ownership of businesses, associations with companies, financial transactions, and in changes in behavior. One reason for the criminal record check is to pick up on serious financial and job performance problems. Those problems can in turn lead to stealing both financial and intellectual assets from the company. An executive or key technological officer becomes a prime target for recruitment as an industrial spy when plagued by financial and personal dilemmas. (Please see *Investigating Computer Crime: A Primer for Security Managers* by Ronald Mendell, Charles C Thomas, 1998, for an in-depth discussion of identifying high-risk employees.)

Ideally, a financial asset investigation should be done prior to hiring an individual for a sensitive position. This practice weeds out undesirables with serious financial problems or business conflicts, and it also provides a benchmark with which to compare subsequent routine checks. Again, the object is not to run a totalitarian state but to carry on routine financial background checks to protect all concerned. With modern electronic databases, these checks are quick and unobtrusive.

SUMMARY

At the advanced level consider whether other "deep pockets" may have liability. Even if your target is penniless, their employer or principal may not be. Develop wage or earning information on the target through public records and by estimation techniques. Use governmental records of regulatory agencies to gain financial data. And finally, take a second look at real estate records and lawsuits involving the subject. You may uncover hidden ties between the subject and others. Discovering improper real estate transactions is also possible. Verify assets and liabilities in financial statements given to mortgage lenders. They may be bogus or overvalued. If the subject's net worth is out of line with previous earnings, look for unreported income.

Chapter 7

FINDING HIDDEN ASSETS

Finding hidden assets is an intriguing topic. It is about the games people play to keep their money out of the hands of creditors. Rarely are the assets found in a tin can buried in the subject's backyard. Most likely, you will not need a shovel. However, a nose for looking beyond the surface of a financial document will come in handy. Financial investigators get paid to rock the boat, to question things that on the surface look just fine. When a subject who is a financial "player" gets cooperative in providing information, do not relax. Be as suspicious as hell. This does not mean making false accusations. It does mean undertaking extensive digging for the truth. When someone tells you how poor they are, research it until you are convinced too. A cynical view of human nature is not necessary; though, confirming what the subject says to be true speaks to the heart of the mission.

USING DISCOVERY TECHNIQUES

Effective searching for hidden assets requires your client educating you properly in advance. They should provide copies of any depositions given by the subject. They should supply copies of any Answers to Interrogatories. Any previous financial reports, investigative reports, and financial documents need reviewing. The depositions or statements of any associates of the subject require reading. If any of the above documents do not exist, the investigator should assist the attorney in preparing questions for discovery. The key points to include in depositions and interrogatories are:

1. Basic Identifiers on the Subject. (You would be surprised at the number of attorneys that omit this information in taking depositions.)
2. Address History on the Subject.
3. Request a copy of the Subject's current Financial Statement.

4. Obtain a Written Authorization to gain access to the person's Credit History.
5. Request a list of Bank Accounts with Balance information.
6. Request a list of all Securities and Negotiable Instruments.
7. Request a list of all Annuities and Life Insurance Policies.
8. Request Travel documents such as Passports, Visas, and Airplane Tickets.
9. A copy of all Credit Card Statements.
10. A copy of Telephone Bills for the last year.
11. Income Tax Records for the last five years.
12. A List of all Businesses in which the subject is an Owner or Manager.

Do not expect the subject to be completely truthful when responding to discovery in aid of a judgment. However, even falsehoods provide a starting place for an investigation. Adopt the attitude of trying to prove every "fact" presented by the subject. Accept as a working hypothesis that the person is telling the truth. In trying to prove a falsehood true, you will discover where, why, and how it is false. Then, it should become clear what the individual wanted to remain buried.

COMMON HIDING PLACES

In mystery novels the main hiding place for secret cash is the wall safe at the home or office. Some stories allude to the loot being stored on the yacht in the harbor. Or perhaps, the leg of the sofa contains the secreted funds. Actual financial hiding places are far more mundane. Not that real debtors lack imagination, but they desire to have their money working for them. It needs to be earning interest or appreciating in value. Most of the hiding places of fiction offer neither of these opportunities. Fortunately for investigators, this need to earn limits the field of deception somewhat.

The most common hiding places for assets are:

1. Home Mortgage Paydown.
2. Universal Life Insurance or Annuity.
3. Purchases of Savings Bonds, Cashier's Checks, and Traveler's Checks.

4. Limited Partnerships.
5. Dissolved Corporations.
6. Stockbroker Accounts.
7. Collectibles.
8. Safe Deposit Boxes.
9. Offshore/Foreign Accounts.
10. Assets in Other Names.
11. Payments to IRS.
12. Sweetheart Lawsuits.

THE PAYDOWN

The Home Mortgage Paydown is a favorite tactic in states like Texas that have a strong homestead protection in their debt collection laws. By applying a large cash payment against the mortgage balance, the debtor hides the cash in the home's equity. Hopefully, the collectors will not check the mortgage balance history, and the debtor emerges from a bankruptcy, or judgment collection effort, with his or her cash intact. Since debtors use the "paydown" in the face of extreme financial difficulties, like legal proceedings, do not hesitate to utilize subpoenas on the subject's mortgage company to obtain the payment history.

If the case is not in litigation, try trash surveillance. It may reveal bank or mortgage statements. If permissible under the Fair Credit Reporting Act, checking the subject's credit history may uncover the transaction. Or, if the subject has Uniform Commercial Code (UCC) filings for mechanic's liens (new roof, additions, swimming pool) that he pays off prematurely, that might be a type of paydown to increase his equity position. Checking the UCC documents indexes at the Secretary of State's office *and* at the county clerk should uncover this practice.

LIFE INSURANCE

Universal life insurance requires an initial investment by the insured to create a fund to pay life insurance policy premiums. Then, each month the insured contributes a regular premium payment to the fund. After monthly deductions for administrative and insurance costs, the remainder of the payment goes into the cash value of the policy where it gathers interest. The concept behind the policy is that it provides life insurance while building surrender value. A besieged debtor can take advantage of the provision in the policy that allows *additional payments* by the insured to the policy fund.

Annuities are an investment program where the purchaser makes a lump sum payment, monthly payments, or both to secure an income in the future. In other words, the debtor can effectively hide cash within these types of policies. They also have the added appeal of being exempt against creditor actions in some states.

When the debtor is in bankruptcy proceedings, they normally have to list all of their life insurance and annuity policies. The investigator should see that the records of all life insurance companies, listed as having policies for the debtor, receive a proper subpoena. All transactional records found for any universal life policies and annuities need review by an accountant or life insurance expert.

In civil cases the same applies for life insurance policies listed in the debtor's Answers to Interrogatories in Aid of Judgment. If a case is not in litigation, obtaining bank statements through the trash, or by a confidential source, could reveal monthly electronic deductions (identifying the insurance company). It may even disclose a recent large cash transfer to the universal life or annuity fund.

The investigator may wish, if legally permissible, to run a credit report to identify where the target obtained recent bank loans. If one has a contact in the banking sector, perhaps obtaining a copy of a financial statement the target used for a loan is possible. The statement may list as an asset the cash value of the policy.

Of course, the investigator should always be on guard for universal life or annuity policies taken out in relatives" names. If they are not listed in the debtor's financial statement for a loan, the investigator will need detailed bank statements and copies of checks to reconstruct the paper trail.

MONEY ORDERS AND OTHER NEGOTIABLE INSTRUMENTS

Bank statements usually will document large purchases of savings bonds, traveler's checks, and cashier's checks. Even if the target purchases postal money orders, or checks and bonds at another bank, the money almost always has to originate from their own checking or savings account. A subpoena to the bank should produce copies of checks for large amounts payable to cash or to the bank. The teller's stamp on the check indicates a transaction at the window.

Cross-checking against the teller's work for that day will reveal any money orders, savings bonds, cashier's checks, and traveler's checks issued. Remember that banks typically microfilm the teller's daily work and any processed checks for large amounts to protect themselves. They also must comply with the microfilming requirements of the federal Bank Secrets Act.

If the investigator suspects large regular purchases of commercial money orders at retail stores, surveillance of the target to the involved locations may be necessary. Regular visits at the same time of the month may indicate covert payments to an annuity or investment account in another state. The same goes for regular purchases of postal money orders. Supplementing the foot surveillance by examining the subject's trash for money order receipts may be necessary. Execute a subpoena on the bank of record for the money orders or on the post office, if needed.

The purchases of savings bonds will probably take place at the subject's local bank. Since customers purchase them at the teller's window for the most part, interviewing bank personnel may be essential to learn about the extent of the transactions. If the subject purchases savings bonds through payroll deduction, copies of their payroll stubs should reveal the details of how much and how often.

LIMITED PARTNERSHIPS

Limited Partnerships are an investment device. The party wanting to raise capital for a business (the general partner) sells limited partnerships to investors. These investors have no legal liability for the debts of the business beyond the amount of their investment. The important restriction on the limited partners is that they may not take an active role in running the business. If they do, they may lose their protection as limited partners. Limited Partnerships (LP's) are not subject to direct taxation by the IRS. The general partner and the limited partners pay income tax on their individual returns. LP's must register in the state where they form. In Texas, for example, the LP files its certificate with the Secretary of State.

These legal entities are great places to hide assets. First, friends or relatives can invest the target's money for him as limited partners. Second, LP's are not usually subject to quick liquidation. Money, once invested, could remain there for long periods of time, maybe years. This factor hinders rapid collection efforts by creditors.

Run the target's name and those of associates in the corporate record section of your Secretary of State's office to obtain LP information. Use Prentice-Hall Online or a similar service to detect LP's in other jurisdictions. Once you identify the LP's, get a copy of their registration certificate. Since the law treats LP's like securities, your state's Registrar of Securities may have additional informational filings on the partnership. Once you obtain all these documents, turn them over to the supervising attorney in the case. They may wish to bring in an accountant to guide you in further investigation.

The accountant may instruct you to investigate whether the subject really was a limited partner. Sometimes general partners masquerade as limited partners. Interviews with former employees of the LP can tell you the role the subject played in the business. Demonstrating that the subject took an active role in the operation of the LP could strip them of their legal protection as a limited partner. Obtaining documents such as UCC filings showing the subject's signature as an operating officer of the LP will help. This sort of evidence also proves that the listed limited partner who is a relative of the subject is not the de facto partner.

DEAD AND DISSOLVED CORPORATIONS

Dissolved corporations are another great place to hide assets. Why? Once most people see that a corporate name is on the dead list at the Secretary of State's office, they put it out of their mind. However, the assets acquired during the term of that corporation may be very much alive. The rule of thumb is to include in property searches, vehicle searches, and searches for other assets the names of any discovered dead or dissolved corporations. You may turn up a significant asset.

Do not underestimate a debtor's resourcefulness. A dead corporation could continue to acquire assets for years after it legally becomes defunct. The automobile he or she drives could be in the old corporate name. The same goes for the boat, the recreational vehicle, or the "condo."

STOCKBROKERS

Stockbroker accounts may contain securities held in the firm's name. Bearer bonds, cash, mutual funds, and other investment vehicles can comprise a portfolio. Investigators may stumble over account reports or financial statements listing securities through searching the trash. However, anytime that you can supply a client a detailed list of securities, owned by a target, consider it the exception to the rule. Frequently, identifying the brokerage firm either by surveillance or by pretext will be the best you can do. Once you identify the broker, your supervising attorney should take it from there. They can use subpoena and discovery methods to flesh out the details from the stockbroker.

COLLECTIBLES AND SAFE DEPOSIT BOXES

Collectibles are difficult to hide. If a subject is an art collector, a numismatist, a baseball card enthusiast, or a philatelist, a good background check will tell you. Scanning local newspapers' databases may reveal an article about the subject's hobby or interest. Interviewing neighbors and associates may provide the necessary background. Putting forward the pretext of being a collector yourself helps. Remember, people are proud of their collections. They like to tell others about them. They love to show them off.

Profiles on a subject in professional journals or in the business press could supply the needed hobby or collector information. Looking for articles, or even classified ads, by the subject in hobbyist or collector magazines may yield useful data. Consider checking the local newspapers for classified ads regarding the subject's collection.

Once you identify the hobby or type of collection, the local stamp club, coin collectors association, or similar group will help in establishing the value. Remember that most collectors want their peers to know the extent of their holdings. Again, ads in periodicals and news-papers may disclose the needed information.

Even before you think about getting a peek at the subject's safe deposit box, intelligent guessing about its contents can occur. Correlating the subject's visits to the box before or after coin or stamp fairs tells you where he keeps his collection. Visits just before a major purchase reveal he keeps cash in the box. Trips to the box after for-eign travel may indicate he or she is transferring funds from offshore or overseas banks. Long sessions in the "clipping rooms" at the vault, coupled with an immediate deposit at the teller's window, inform you where the subject keeps the coupon bonds.

Close surveillance is useful in determining the above facts. However, if feasible, gathering information from bank tellers and vault attendants will enhance the investigation. Effective pretext interviews of the bank's staff, done in a low-key manner, will make some head-way. They can relate the frequency and types of transactions per-formed by the subject. These are entry-level positions with reasonably high turnover rates. Placing people in the bank to support a major case may also fill the information gaps.

Investigators should consider trying to discover the name of the target's accountant. Records from civil lawsuits, especially copies of income tax records produced by the target, may lead you to the name. The client attorney, armed with this information, can subpoena the accounting firm and its records for a deposition. This action alone could root out a great deal of banking data.

OVERSEAS OR OFFSHORE ACCOUNTS AND BUSINESSES

Many investigators hit a stone wall when they learn a subject has overseas or offshore accounts and businesses. Languages, differences in laws and customs, and outright secrecy pose new problems. However, English language resources about foreign banks and busi-nesses do exist. An investigator should find out if the local university has a specialty library for the region in question. For example, in a recent investigation on a Puerto Rican company, I discovered the University of Texas at Austin has a Latin American Studies library. I found several reference works in English providing basic information about the company.

Providing information very similar to the *Million Dollar Directory,* the Dun's guides cover Latin America and other regions around the globe. For example, one can consult the guide, *Europe's 10,000 Largest Companies.* An investigator can use Matthew Lesko's guide to U.S. governmental resources, *Information USA,* to find the names of foreign country experts in the Department of Commerce. These individuals can supply details of where one can find business information for individual countries anywhere in the world. Calling on these experts is akin to having a high-powered, paid specialist for the mere cost of a telephone conversation.

Another resource to consider is the array of electronic business databases discussed in Chapter 8. While many of businesses covered by DIALOG's databases will be American, those companies may be the owners of the foreign businesses you are researching. The databases also provide information on foreign-owned businesses here in the U.S.A.

Leonard Fuld's *Competitor Intelligence* has a chapter on locating foreign business information. His book suggests these resources as starting points:

1. Securities Brokers with expertise on foreign businesses.
2. The International Trade Commission.
3. International Trade Shows.
4. Foreign Consulates. (He supplies a list.)
5. Foreign Chambers of Commerce. (Again, he lists.)
6. Foreign Magazines and Directories. (He lists the key business publications for each major country.)

For background information on foreign banks, Fuld suggests checking publications like *Euromoney 500* for profiles on the world's top 500 banks. *The Europa Year Book* also provides basic data on banks around the world. Major foreign banks have offices in New York City which may provide some background information on their home-base operations. When an investigator learns that a subject uses a particular foreign bank, knowing as much about the bank is essential to the success of the investigation.

One can enhance the depth of the research by running the bank's name on a CD-ROM disk of a national newspaper like *The Washington Times* or *The New York Times.* Such a search will produce a list of all articles for the last year on the bank in question. If your computer does not have CD-ROM capability, try using Information Access Company's general and business periodical indexes, under the label of InfoTrac, at a major public library. What one can learn about a foreign bank or business using these resources is quite frankly invaluable. Foreign correspondents with in-depth knowledge of the bank or business in question may supply detailed information with a telephone call. Otherwise, they can supply solid background information on that country's banking system and privacy laws.

Running searches under the name of the country such as the "Cayman Islands" combined with terms like "banking" or "finance" may provide insightful articles. One time, I ran a search on *The Washington Times* index on CD-ROM (Published by Wayzata Technology, 1993) using the subject "money laundering." I learned about how American companies were hiding funds in foreign subsidiaries. They invoiced themselves $100 for an item that cost a mere dollar.

The money would go into the accounts of their foreign company. It could undergo laundering or re-investment there without paying taxes on it here. I received general confirmation of what I suspected a Texas-based company was doing with its Mexican subsidiary. After obtaining copies of invoices from the Texas business by way of the trash, I was able to establish what was going on. If you desire further ideas about investigative techniques, the *IRS Special Agent's Guide to the Money Laundering Control Act of 1986* is helpful. You can obtain a copy from a Federal Depository Library at your local state university.

Using the OCLC or RLIN (see Chap. 3) and the *Directory of Special Libraries and Information Centers* could lead you to some special collections on foreign banks and businesses. In doing my research on a business in Puerto Rico, I used OCLC to uncover a Congressional report entitled "Money Laundering in Puerto Rico." While my inquiry did not focus on illegal activities, I did find the report very useful in explaining the banking system in Puerto Rico. If you run into a printed source in a foreign language, library staff can assist in brief translations to gain access to statistical information or data about a business.

In certain cases, even after extensive research on your part, bringing in an investigative specialist on foreign banks and businesses is necessary. Investigative organizations such as the National Association of Legal Investigators or the World Association of Detectives are sources for specialists on overseas or offshore asset searches. To aid a specialist, the investigator may want, if the case is in litigation, the deposition taken of the target. A subpoena duces tecum to the subject should require that they bring their passport, telephone records, and credit card and bank statements. The documents will provide important clues as to the location of foreign assets. If the case is not in litigation, the investigator can gather similar documents and information through trash and close surveillance, interviews with associates, public records research, and periodical research. The investigator could consider pretext calls to the subject's travel agent and business associates.

Finally, while this sounds odd, an effective way to acquire a subject's foreign business or banking information may involve sending them a check. If the person runs a business involving any kind of mail order, buying a small item with a check will result in receiving the cancelled check back in one's bank statement. I did this with an individual that ran a newsletter. The check I sent returned with the name of his Costa Rican bank stamped on the back.

If the subject does not engage in a mail-order business, sending a small "refund check" from a business will do the trick. The reverse of this technique is to send an announcement of a new newsletter of interest to the subject. Request a nominal sum for a charter subscription. Upon receipt of the check, even if drawn on an American bank, an investigator would have the banking information to begin the paper trail search. One could mail the check back, uncashed, explaining there was not sufficient interest in the proposed newsletter.

OTHER FINANCIAL DODGES

Assets in other names will always be the bane of the financial investigator's existence. However, do not assume the subject will be highly creative. If in the preliminary investigation you find the names of the immediate relatives, especially the spouse, the majority of the battle is over. Be consistent in running these immediate family members' names. Though, be on the lookout for the unusual: the nephew or cousin whose name appears in the public record more often than it should.

As strange as it sounds, the IRS may be a good place to hide cash. Deliberate overpayments of quarterly taxes offer a quick, safe place. Recouping the money at the end of the year in a refund is not difficult.

Careful examination of bank statements, checks and checkbooks, and subpoenaed tax returns should reveal this practice. Again, forensic examination by an accountant may be necessary.

Sweetheart Lawsuits

The "sweetheart" lawsuit escapes the notice of many lawyers and investigators. Think of it as a bogus liability. The last chapter discussed bogus assets. Bogus liabilities also work to the advantage of debtors. Most people figure that the existence of a lawsuit means the parties involved have opposing interests. Usually, this perception is correct. In our culture we tend to view being sued as a totally negative event. But, it can offer several advantages to those with "financial challenges."

An entrepreneur takes on considerable debt in starting a business. This enterprise begins to fail. Creditors want their money. How does one keep the wolves away from the assets? The entrepreneur gets a friend to sue the business for a large sum under some kind of pretext. It may require concocting a secured loan agreement or contract which then goes into "default." The defendant in the subsequent lawsuit employs only a token defense resulting in a large judgment by the plaintiff. If the business goes into bankruptcy, a large portion of the liquidated assets goes to this "creditor." The money then gets recycled to the debtor after an appropriate handling fee for the phony creditor.

Bogus lawsuits help to shield defendants against other creditors. When faced with a possible real lawsuit, they come forward and say something like, "I'd pay you people but I cannot afford it. Look, I got another judgment against me for $600,000 and I can't pay that. Sue me and I'll just file for bankruptcy." One large sweetheart lawsuit can run interference against legitimate claims for years.

Lawsuits assist in attempts to defraud a third party. Two parties agree to an action where one claims injury caused by the other. No one was actually injured, but a setup of a solvent third party or insurance company occurs to get a payoff. This type of case falls more in the realm of insurance fraud investigation. However, it deserves noting because of the greed it engenders. People that defraud insurance companies will not bat an eye at defrauding a creditor. Look out for this type of behavior when reviewing a subject's litigation history.

When you suspect possible sweetheart lawsuits, obtain a full litigation history on the target. Go beyond the cases listed in the target's Answers to Interrogatories. They may not be completely truthful on listing all previous lawsuits. Check the civil lawsuit databases at the county, statewide, and federal level. You may have to use an information broker (see Chap. 4) or a service like CDB Infotek to check statewide. Do nationwide searches with these services when you suspect actions in other jurisdictions.

Whenever possible, obtain a copy or examine the courthouse file for each action. Review each file carefully. Is there any pattern of repeating defendants or plaintiffs? Do the facts of the cases sound similar? Was a default judgment taken? Or, was a judgment taken because the defendant failed to respond to discovery?

Do you find a thin file, with an agreed judgment for a large amount, completed not long after the commencement of the suit? Are the names of the same lawyers coming up again and again?

A comparison with the subject's credit file may reveal that large lawsuits have a habit of appearing when he or she can no longer make the payments to legitimate creditors. Interviews with past judgment creditors may reveal whether the lawsuit was on the "up and up." People with a legitimate judgment against a defendant will be glad to trade information with you. It may help them get their money. If you meet stonewalling instead or if you get referred to their attorney, get suspicious. Become even more suspicious when their attorney has no comment. Remember, these people are supposed to be adversaries. When they treat a potential ally as an enemy and the defendant as a friend, something is wrong.

SUMMARY

Hiding assets is a game. The skillful players try to place assets in the names of relatives or associates. They may also use defunct corporations as hiding places. Effective asset searches require background investigations on the target's ties to other people and businesses. Old business names need checking for existing ownership of assets like boats, vehicles, and property.

Complex methods of camouflage may include the use of limited partnerships, of stockbroker accounts, of offshore and foreign accounts, and even of overpayments to the IRS. Closely working with your client attorney and a Certified Public Accountant may be essential in such cases. Identifying the target's own accountant will provide additional help to your legal team since this individual can be deposed for detailed information.

Finally, the investigator should not overlook mundane hiding places like collectibles, safe deposit boxes, or home mortgage pay-downs. Life insurance policies, annuities, and the purchases of cashier's checks, money orders, traveler's checks, and savings bonds should also be considered. Using the Hidden Assets Form (Form 4) will help organize the data.

Form 4

Hidden Assets Form

Case: Date:

Subject:

Basic Identifiers:

Names of Key Relatives, Associates, and Friends:

Leads gained from Review of Discovery Materials:

Banking Information:
[Cross-reference Banking Summary Chapter 11]

Checklist:

1. Home Mortgage Paydown:

    Name of Institution _____
    History of Payments Obtained [ ]
    UCCs Checked [ ]

2. Universal Life or Annuity:

    Companies _____
    History of Contributions Obtained [ ]

3. Savings Bonds, Cashier's Checks, Money Orders, and Traveler's Checks/ Safe Deposit Boxes:

    Cross-reference against Banking Summary [ ]
    Surveillance [ ]

Form 4

Continued

4. Limited Partnerships/Dead and Dissolved Corporations:

   Check at Secretary of State [ ]
   Ran Names for Assets [ ]

5. Stockbroker:

   Trash Surveillance [ ]
   Financial Records Review [ ]

6. Collectibles:

   Background Research [ ]
   Interviews [ ]

7. Offshore/Foreign Businesses and Accounts:

   Background Research [ ]
   Review of Discovery [ ]

8. Assets-In-Other-Names:

   Association Summary [ ]

9. Overpayments to IRS:

   Banking Records [ ]
   Deposition of Accountant [ ]

10. Sweetheart Lawsuits:

    Local Courthouse Research [ ]
    State-wide Database Research [ ]
    Nation-wide Database Research [ ]

Chapter 8

BASIC BUSINESS ASSET SEARCH

This chapter presents the basic building blocks of a business asset search. It starts with scanning for fundamental business data. The process continues with completing the target's business profile, getting commercial credit reports, obtaining SEC reports, and securing personal property renderings.

The text then explains how to integrate the results of individual asset searches into the business search. Forms 5 (Business Profile) and 8 (Business Asset Summary) provide the means to record the gathered data.

The Basic Business Asset Search does raise its own unique questions. First introduced in Chapter 4, the business search deals with the fundamental questions concerning a business: What type of legal structure does it have? When was it formed? Who are the principal owners or officers? What are its principal product lines or services? How many people does it employ? What are its annual sales?

The answers serve as keys. If a business is a corporation, the Secretary of State will have an incorporation file. Examining that file will lead to discovering the date of incorporation, the names of officers, incorporators, the registered agent, and the number of initial shares. The discovered names may evolve into individual searches for background data. Having the incorporation date will set a benchmark for searching historical and public records. The number of shares at inception may offer insight into the company's capitalization.

Knowing the company's major product lines opens a multitude of information sources. Suppliers, vendors, and customers become easier to identify. One can research the literature on the economics and finances of that particular industry. Trade publications, professional journals, and governmental reports all tell about the health of that product line, and even of the targeted company.

Uncovering the annual sales figures creates data for calculating other important financial numbers. Chapter 10 will explain the use of key business ratios to figure liabilities and assets from sales dollars. Getting the fundamental questions answered provides the basis for more advanced research.

ADDITIONAL FINANCIAL PARAMETERS

Other important questions about a business worth pondering include: How does cash flow in and out of the business? Who does the company's banking? What is the condition of the business's balance sheet?

An investigator answers the first question by identifying the persons and organizations that bring funds into the company's front door. From interviewing these customers and clients, one learns the goods and services provided by the target. Typically, they provide answers to the following: Do they pay the target with cash or by check? What are the other possible payment arrangements? Is there a system of loan payments, discounted purchases, or rebates? What bank are the target's refund checks drawn on?

Those taking money out of the business (suppliers and vendors) will provide similar data. Parties on both sides of the cash flow equation may have knowledge about the target's annual sales and balance sheet data. Much of this information comes from the sources with the use of a simple telephone pretext. Start off by saying, "XYZ Company would like to buy widgets from my company. I understand they purchase gadgets from you. What is their payment history?" The remainder of the conversation normally falls into place. Educating yourself about the supplier or vendor is the key. Research them in a trade directory before calling (see the "Business Sources" section in Chapter 4). That way, you can talk their "talk" (see "Interviewing Techniques" in Chapter 10).

Balance Sheets

To compute a balance sheet, gather together all the asset and liability data from public records and from interviews. The application of key business ratios (discussed in Chapter 10) could prove helpful in estimating unknown figures. The fundamental principle of accounting dictates that the ASSETS of a business must equal the SUM of the LIABILITIES and the OWNER'S EQUITY. To better understand this concept, looking at the mortgage on a building would be a good example. The market value of the building is $100,000. That figure goes into the ASSETS column. The existing mortgage is $70,000 which goes into the LIABILITIES column. If the owner sells the building, he or she gets to keep $30,000, the OWNER'S EQUITY or stake in the building. By adding the liability and equity figures together, one sees that they equal the asset value.

In crafting a rough balance sheet, the investigator places all the known market values of assets together. Liabilities like debts and mortgages compose the other side of the balance sheet. If one subtracts the liabilities from the assets, the result is the owner's equity or net worth of the business. The obvious targets for collection efforts are businesses with sufficient net worth to satisfy the pending debt. The trick lies in making sure both the asset and liability figures accurately reflect reality.

SCANNING FOR INFORMATION

Begin with the simple sources; the sources that are under your nose. Analyze the company's ad in the local yellow pages. Check the local newspaper for other advertisements by the business. The employment classifieds describe expansion plans, new products, and even financial details about the firm. They reveal what types of jobs they have open and the extent of the compensation packages. Examining the microfilm over a period of months or years could explain the history of the company's growth.

The local Better Business Bureau may have a file detailing the company's history, business rating, and complaint record. The names of similar businesses (other automobile dealers, retail stores, air conditioning contractors, etc.) may be available. They could serve as leads for background information on the target.

Consider doing some fundamental library research. Run the name of the business on the local newspaper's database (available at the public library or the local university library's reference section) to obtain any articles concerning the enterprise. The county or city history center may have historical records pertaining to the business: a collection of past city directories, telephone books, and newspaper clippings piecing together the company's history. As an added bonus, the history center may have the names of professional or trade organizations where the target or its employees belong. Contact with those organizations may provide useful information on the target's history, ownership, size, and financial strength.

Your local public library's business information center may have a collection of local business directories which provide basic biographical and statistical information. Statewide and national directories of businesses found at the library are another excellent resource. Chapter 4 discussed the *Directory of Texas Manufacturers* (published annually), Dun and Bradstreet's *Million Dollar Directory,* the *Thomas Register of Manufacturers,* and Dun's Business Identification Service microfiche which briefly describes over ten million companies.

Whenever an investigator needs to learn the names of other business directories for a given field, they need to refer to *Directories in Print* by Gale Research. Another valuable research tool is Lorna M. Daniells's *Business Information Sources.* It describes a wide range of U.S. and foreign business reference works. *Ward's Business Directory of U.S. Private and Public Companies* by Gale Research is an excellent adjunct to the directories mentioned above. It provides basic product line information about a large number of privately owned companies.

The business editor of the city newspaper may direct you to persons with an in-depth knowledge about the company. Also, consider the chamber of commerce as a possible resource. The targeted business may have ads or articles in the local chamber of commerce's publication. In addition, the chamber may publish profiles of certain local industries, supplying overall statistical information, with a possible spotlight on the target firm. If the local business newspaper or magazine ran an article on the target, talk to the reporter who wrote it.

If the target business operates outside of your locality, use nationwide newspaper databases such as NEXIS, DataTimes, National Newspaper Index, and InfoTrac. In addition, databases such as Interstate Public Filings, Business Public Filings, CDB Infotek and Information America need scanning when possible national business interests become a factor. Of course, for publicly owned companies, the Disclosure/Spectrum database provides search capability through DIALOG. LEXIS also offers access to Securities and Exchange Commission (SEC) filings.

One may also consult the other DIALOG business databases mentioned in Chapter 4. If one needs details about additional business databases, consulting the *Directory of Online Databases* by Cuadra

Associates will provide hundreds of sources. It is updated semi-annually to keep you abreast of the information explosion. New databases are "popping up" all the time.

CD-ROMs

An investigator should not overlook what business information is on CD-ROM. Three reference books which list what is available include:

1. The *Encyclopedia of Business Information Sources* by Gale Research (1988) contains listings by topic of many reference works in print and on CD-ROM of interest to investigators.

2. *CD-ROMs in Print* by Meckler in Westport, CT publishes an annual (1987-1992) description of information available in this format.

3. *Directories in Print,* 1993, by Gale Research, lists any commercial directories in print, microform, and in CD-ROM formats.

Expect this new medium for storing information to grow at an explosive rate for the foreseeable future. An excellent introduction to the topic is the book, *Welcome . . . to CD-ROM* by Tom Benford (MIS Press, 1993). He explains the technology in detail without getting bogged down in technical jargon.

In addition to local and national newspapers being on CD-ROM, investigators should note these other new sources:

1. Phonedisc USA, the Reverse Edition. This five-disc set allows searching ninety million business and residential telephone listings by name, address, telephone number, or type of business. It is a good source for finding a targeted business's multiple locations and is available through TigerSoftware (800-888-4437).

2. Lesko's Information USA (Info-Power) by INFOBUSINESS. This is a guide to U.S. government business-related information. It is also available on CD-ROM from TigerSoftware.

3. USGPO Monthly Catalog of U.S. Government Publications. This disc indexes the U.S. Government Printing Office's output of publications and is a good resource to check when doing background research on an industry or product. Available at university libraries.

4. Investext. A full text of corporate and industry analyses on CD-ROM. Found at university libraries.

OTHER BASIC BUSINESS REFERENCE SOURCES

The following may offer basic data about a business or industry:

1. *United States Industrial Outlook* provides the federal government's predictions on how 350 manufacturing and service industries will fare in the upcoming year. Published annually in December, it supplies basic statistics about each industry. It is a good background book by which one can judge the performance of the targeted business by industry norms.

2. *How to Find Information About Companies* by Washington Researchers has many tips on how to locate public records on small and medium-sized companies.

3. *The Dow Jones-Irwin Business and Investment Almanac* is published annually by Dow Jones-Irwin. It contains extensive information on stocks, SEC filings, mutual funds, and definitions of important financial terms. In addition, it has a guide to online business databases and a directory of other business sources.

4. *Business Information: How to Find It, How to Use It* by Michael Lavin is another good source to consult when stumped about how to develop information about a company.

5. The *Rand McNally International Bankers Directory* is a fine source for getting basic information on over fifteen thousand U.S. banks. It is useful when trying to develop banking leads from UCC filings or motor vehicle title liens.

6. Your state government's organizational manual will explain how to locate state agencies that might have records pertaining to the targeted company. These records can range from license application to legislative and regulatory hearings.

All the information gathered so far should answer the fundamental business questions posed at the beginning of the chapter. By posting these answers on the Business Profile (Form 5), in most cases, a basic understanding of the target's business will emerge. However, small businesses and non-profit organizations may create exceptions to relatively easy fact gathering.

STATE FILING REQUIREMENTS

All profit and not-for-profit corporations must register with the Secretary of State, or its equivalent, in your jurisdiction. A database

Form 5

Business Profile

Case: Subject: Date:

Corporate Name: Charter Number:

Type: Date Founded:

Number of Employees: Annual Sales:

Principal Product or Service Lines: Primary SIC Codes:

Officers/Directors: Registered Agent:

Principal Locations: Where Incorporated?

Owns or Owned By: Number of Shares?

Location of Bank Accounts:

Sources of Available Funds:

Cash Flow Profile:

Net Worth from Balance Sheet Analysis:

---

check at that agency should produce officer/director data, the name of the registered agent, the date of incorporation, and the type of corporation: domestic profit, non-profit, or foreign. Record this information on Form 5 and cross-reference it on Form 8. Limited Partnerships should also be registered at the Secretary of State level. Record them on the same forms as for corporations. However, be sure to document which persons are limited partners and which are general partners.

It is critical to research every dead corporation or limited partnership that your target business previously operated. Cross-reference them on Form 8. As indicated in Chapter 7, such entities tend to become hiding places for assets and cash. Run their names, too, when checking for vehicles, boats, aircraft, and real estate.

Unincorporated Businesses

Sole proprietorships and ordinary partnerships present the greatest research challenge. By scanning the Assumed Name filing database at the county clerk's office, one can learn the names of owners and partners, addresses, and date of filing. Since most businesses have to pay or collect some kind of state tax, the state-level taxing authority should have some ownership information about the targeted business. When I reach my rope's end regarding the ownership of a small business, the Texas Comptroller of Public Accounts' Sales Tax database generally bails me out. With a simple telephone call, this agency tells me the names of the company's owners and the locations around the state. A similar resource will exist in your jurisdiction.

The U.S. Post Office must reveal ownership information of businesses with post office boxes. Postal mailing permits obtained by such businesses are subject to Freedom of Information Act (FOIA) requests. By doing an FOIA request to the central post office in that city, an investigator can obtain a copy of the business's permit application.

Another overlooked place for information on small businesses is the city building code department or zoning commission. If the business is a contractor, it may need a city license. If it needed office space built or remodeled, it had to obtain city permits. If it wanted a zoning variance, it had to fill out an application.

Charitable and Non-Profit Organizations

Non-profit organizations listed on the Internal Revenue Service's *Cumulative List of Organizations* must file a financial disclosure form 990 with the IRS. The organization must make available for public inspection at their offices the last three years of its form 990 filings. Usually, the organization will provide a copy by mail. Private foundations must file a form 990-PF which is also public.

Checking with the Attorney General's Charitable Fraud Division in your state may be very useful when investigating questionable fund-raising organizations. If a "charity" has a track record of deceptive trade practices and debt dodging, making an open-record request on the file could save a lot of legwork. The Better Business Bureau maintains files on "shady" charitable organizations and "non- profit" groups. In addition, they could direct you to local or regional watchdog groups that might have extensive information on the target. Watchdog groups are especially useful when investigating the finances of extremist political or religious organizations that claim charitable or non-profit status.

BUSINESS CREDIT REPORTS

Experian business credit reports are available on the information service CompuServe for about thirteen million businesses. Information brokers who belong to Dun and Bradstreet can offer access to credit reports on over nine million businesses. Credit reports provide brief background data on a business such as name, address, standard industrial classification, the age of the firm, and any parent or subsidiary companies. In addition, they contain some financial figures like annual sales or net worth. And just like any credit report, they will have the business's payment record. Additionally, interviews with suppliers and vendors will provide indirect information on creditworthiness. Record credit information on Form 6.

SEC REPORTS

The SEC publishes annually the *Directory of Companies Required to File Annual Reports with the Securities and Exchange Commission.* (Major public libraries and university libraries have a copy.) If it lists your target, then you will want to examine their 10-K (annual) and 10-Q (quarterly) reports through LEXIS's Federal Securities Library. The Disclosure database through DIALOG has extracts of 10-K's, 10-Q's, and 20-F financial reports. The S-1, a new registrant's report, is also available through Disclosure. Many public libraries offer annual reports by both national and local companies in hard copy and on microfiche. Of course, one may check SEC ONLINE on CD-ROM at a university library.

Form 6

Business Credit

Case: Date:

Subject:

Credit Service: Rating:

Trades:	*Creditor*	*High Bal.*	*Low Bal.*	*Current Bal.*

Basic Background: Locations:

Financials:

Other Information:

OTHER INFORMATION SOURCES (FROM CHAPTER 3)

The following sources were discussed in Chapter 3 and should be a part of the Basic Business Asset Search:

1. Real Property: Grantor/Grantee, Regional Tax Assessing Authority.
2. Vehicles, Boats, Aircraft.
3. UCC Filings.
4. Tax Liens.
5. Civil Suits.
6. Bankruptcy (Chapter 11 case).
7. Corporate Filings.

The connection between the Individual Basic Asset Search and the business one stems from the needs of the client. If the client is primarily concerned with knowing about the individuals involved in a business, then your main emphasis would be on the individual searches, doing enough of a business search to identify the key officers. The converse would be true if the client wanted to know more about the businesses. Finding the appropriate mix for a given client is not difficult. An investigator should place references to individual searches in the cross-reference section of Form 8.

PERSONAL PROPERTY RENDERINGS

One last basic search applicable to businesses is the annual inventory of equipment, inventory, and supplies submitted to the local assessing authority. In Texas, this is called a Personal Property Rendering. The actual inventory listing is confidential. However, you can get the assessed totals for a given year. This is something that can be thrown into the overall financial statement for a business. However, by itself, it does not tell a great deal. A word of caution is in order. Many times the figures are estimates by the assessing authority. Record this information on Form 7.

PIERCING THE CORPORATE VEIL

The law recognizes natural persons and artificial or legal persons such as corporations, estates, and trusts. Generally, a natural person or a group of natural persons seek to limit personal liability by forming a corporation to conduct business. For the most part, these corporations exist for a lawful and ethical purpose. If a group of investors wants to build an office building, they are exercising good business sense by forming a corporation to accomplish the mission. Such a legal move protects the investors from personal liability for the debts of the construction project.

Unfortunately, not all corporations are formed for lawful purposes. Some corporations exist only as an illegal shield against debts and liabilities. In these cases, the corporation often becomes what the law calls an "alter ego" of the individual or persons claiming the benefit of corporate protection. So, the asset investigator may, at times, be forced to examine whether a corporation falls into the "alter ego" category. Ultimately, of course, the determination of alter ego status will lie with the appropriate court of law. An investigator, under an attorney's supervision, will have to gather the evidence, though, necessary for the court's determination. Here are some points to consider in checking a corporation's true personality:

1. The corporation fiction is merely a ploy to perpetrate a fraud. (John wants $10,000 worth of stereo equipment but doesn't want to pay for it. So, he forms a corporation for the sole purpose of buying the equipment in the corporation's name. He has no intention of ever paying the bill.)
2. Corporate formalities have not been observed. (Joe incorporates his business but has no stockholders other than himself. He never keeps any minutes, never holds stockholder meetings, never issues stock, and so on.)
3. Corporate and individual assets are intermixed. (Paul runs his corporation out of his personal checking account. Bills for personal items come in the corporation's name; bills for corporate items come in Paul's name. No line demarcates Paul's finances from the corporate monies.)
4. The corporation and the individual keep the same books, have the same employees, use the same facilities, and use the same stationery.

5. The corporation does not file tax returns.
6. The corporation does not contract consistently in its own name.
7. Purchases of personal property are not for the benefit of the corporation but for the sole benefit of individuals.
8. Shareholders act as if they were partners not like shareholders. (The corporation has no will or destiny of its own. It operates at the whim of one or a few people who are stockholders in name only.)
9. Corporate income and expenditures are not properly accounted for.
10. Use of corporate funds to pay personal expenses of individuals goes on without proper accounting or authorization.
11. The corporation was formed to circumvent personal debts, debts arising from litigation, or a state or federal statute.
12. With officers as just figureheads, they have no say in the corporate operations; the corporation has a sham structure. A silent owner calls all the shots.

Proving a sham corporation involves building a paper trail. An investigator will need to obtain the following documents during the course of his or her inquiry into a possible "alter ego corporation":

A. Receipts, invoices, bills, and other documentation about income and expenses for the corporation for the last year.
B. Corporate income tax records for the last three years.
C. Copies of sales tax, franchise tax, and real property tax records for the last three years.
D. Bank statements, canceled checks, and check registers for the last year for the corporation.
E. Utility records for the corporation for the last year.
F. Copies of leases or mortgages in the name of the corporation.
G. Copies of minutes of the meetings of the board of directors and stockholders' meetings for at least two years prior.
H. The articles of incorporation for the company.
I. Copies of records of stock issued.
J. A copy of the corporation's general ledger for the last year.
K. A current balance sheet and a revenue and expense statement.
L. Copies of a current inventory of the corporation's assets.
M. Copies of any litigation currently involving the corporation filed within the last three years.

N. Copies of any notes payable to the corporation signed by individuals.

O. Copies of all active UCC filings involving the corporation.

Receipts, invoices, and bills may be partially recovered from "dumpster diving" and "trash reconnaissance." (Please check the legality of this practice in your jurisdiction. Also see Chapter 5.) Otherwise, production through legal discovery in a lawsuit will be your only avenue of access. The same holds true for corporate income tax records, bank records, corporate minutes, stock records, the general ledger documents, balance sheets, asset inventories, and notes payable. Unless the target is careless and throws them in the trash, your legal methods will have to be Interrogatories and Requests for Production.

The following may, however, be available as public records:

A. Sales tax, franchise tax, and real property records.
B. Utility records: the utility should at least disclose the name in which the bills are charged.
C. Leases or mortgages may be available from real estate records and by interviewing landlords.
D. Litigation records should be available at the local courthouse.
E. The Secretary of State should have UCC filings.

Piercing the corporate veil is an investigative challenge, but it can be a rewarding case to pursue. Don't forget to interview people whose names come up on the records that you locate. They can provide extensive background information on how the corporation really operates. You can cover the signs or symptoms of "alter ego" corporation with the witness and learn what they observed.

SUMMARY

Using the resources of public and university libraries, scan printed directories of manufacturers and trade associations to gain information about the target. Check the local newspaper and national databases such as NEXIS/LEXIS and CDB Infotek. Research local historical collections and the resources of local business publications for background information. Use the FOIA requests to obtain information from postal authorities on small businesses. Contact the Attorney

General's office and the Better Business Bureau on questionable charities and non-profit organizations.

Integrate the business search with individual searches of officers or owners. Note that several information sources are common to both business and individual searches. Try to learn all the key company names and officers' names early in the process by effective scanning techniques. Then, later, run all the names at each information source for the various types of property and assets. The Basic Business Asset Summary (Form 8) brings together all the business data from the various forms presented in the book.

Form 7

Personal Property Renderings

Case: Date:

Subject:

Year   *Amount in Dollars*

Taxing Authority:

Form 8

Basic Business Asset Summary

Case: Date Commenced:

Subject: Date Completed:

Cross-references to Individual Asset Reports:

Real Property:

Evaluations:

Vehicles:

Boats and Aircraft:

Banking Information:

Form 8

Continued

Business Credit:

Business Profile Information:

Type of Business: Product Lines:

Officers: Where and when incorporated?

Annual Sales?   Number of Employees?

Net Worth?   Cash Flow Profile?

Business Locations:

Visiting the Business:

Form 8

Continued

UCC Filings:

___

Tax Liens:

___

Civil Suits:

___

Bankruptcy:

___

Personal Property Renderings:

___

Chapter 9

THE PLANT VISIT

Visiting the premises of the target business gets the investigator out of the library or from behind the computer screen. They must switch from good research skills to excellent observational abilities. The general guidelines are simple. When in doubt, take photographs of the site. Do not trust your memory to record every detail. Photographs document what the investigator saw; the client gets to look through the investigator's eyes. Take extensive notes; again, do not trust your memory for recalling details like license plates, trucking company names, and delivery times. Finally, do not break any laws, nor cause any confrontations. Keep your visit legal and friendly. You may have to go back later for more information.

The overall aim of visiting a commercial property is to gain names, license plate numbers, and other means of identifying those companies doing business with your target. Additionally, an investigator can confirm whether published reports on the target's number of employees, size of plant, and principal product lines contain accurate data.

This chapter covers specifically what to look for when doing an inspection of the physical premises of a target business. It first presents general things to observe such as the surroundings of the plant, security at the site, and information in the office areas. It also discusses the significance of the size of the parking lots and machinery found in the workyard. Concluding with an explanation of details, the text covers the importance of building size in properly evaluating the site and the target's use of hazardous materials.

THE OVERVIEW

Pay attention to the surroundings. Is the plant located in an urban, suburban, or rural area? What is the economic status of the neighborhood? What kinds of businesses are in the immediate vicinity? Do railroad tracks and special utility lines serve the site? How extensive is the security around the site?

Many factors determine a plant's setting. It may be in a rural area due to land costs. Perhaps, they needed wide open spaces to do product testing. The local area may have cheap labor costs relative to the city. Or, they were closer to a main supplier there. Maybe, they could not afford anything else. Regardless of the locale, try to find out why the target is there. Check with the planning commission, the zoning board, state regulatory agencies, the state employment commission, local utilities, and the chamber of commerce for the answer. Such inquiries will lead to a greater understanding of the economic basis of the firm.

The economic status of the neighborhood tells an investigator much about what a firm can produce. Dirty, heavy industries like metal forges or foundries will not find welcome in upscale business or residential areas. However, a software or computer manufacturer probably would receive a welcoming applause. In addition, the locating of a firm in an upscale area may indicate the business's level of financial success. Reviewing the minutes of the city council could reveal tax breaks granted the business as a lure to come to the community. The business press may have an article on the firm's coming to town.

Businesses like credit unions and car dealerships in the area may tell an investigator about the target business. The credit union may reveal the number of employees of the firm that are members. They could have wage survey information on the business and even general financial background on the company. Financial institutions like credit unions need to know about the companies that employ their membership. If you indicate that you are doing background research, they will most likely share what is publicly available. Nearby car dealerships will know basic financial information about the target business; they want to sell vehicles to its employees. Sales people like to talk. If you approach the topic properly, they may be able to tell a great deal about the target.

Large power lines entering the site indicate a high level of power consumption. Interviewing engineers with the local utility may enlighten you on the equipment at the site requiring large amounts of power. Railroad tracks in current use to the site may mean the use of heavy parts, materials, or supplies.

Site Security

Extensive security at the site could encompass:

1. Perimeter Fencing with Barbed-Wire Roll at the Top.
2. Perimeter Lighting System.
3. Guard Stations at all Entrances.
4. Roving Guard Patrols along the Perimeter.
5. Separate Guard-Controlled Truck Entrances.
6. Additional Exterior Lighting on Buildings.
7. Use of Video Cameras and Alarm Systems.

All of these measures cost money, lots of it. Companies do not spend it on security unless they have a clear need to do so. The employment of extensive security means a company has a large operational budget and has considerable intellectual or physical assets to protect. An investigator may wish to find out the name of the firm's Security Director and check the local business press and Business Periodical Index for articles about him or her. Professional magazines like *Security Management* may have articles written by the director. Such articles may provide the rationale for such security, giving additional financial or economic background on the firm.

Going Inside

A visit to the business may produce promotional materials such as sales brochures or handouts. Frequently, the sales staff will hand you such items with a smile on their face and their ears open to any questions you might have. After all, selling the company and its products are their job. These items and advertising materials may lead to greater understanding of the business's product lines, history, officers and owners. Whenever you need cooperation in getting background information on a business, head for the sales force.

Upon first arriving, make note of any signs or floor directories about the premises. They provide a clue to the identity and location of key officers and departments and to the size of the operation. In the office or reception area, pay attention to anything that could be an information clue:

1. Calendars from suppliers and vendors.
2. Licenses, certificates, and diplomas on the walls.

3. Labels on magazines in the waiting room.
4. Nameplates on desks (possible future sources).
5. Annual reports, company newsletters, in-house bulletins in the waiting room.
6. Company's internal phone book by the telephone used by visitors.
7. OSHA and Worker's Compensation Notices posted on the bulletin board.
8. Markings on file cabinets and file folders that indicate the nature of company operations. ("lawsuits," "overdue bills," etc.)

Parking Lots, Storage Yards, and Delivery Areas

In the parking lot, estimate the number of slots for employees and then for visitors. Then, count the number that are occupied. This should give you a rough idea of the number of employees and the visitor traffic into the plant or office. An additional traffic count at the change of shift at the plant will further substantiate your figures. Write down license plate numbers of vehicles parked in reserved slots for the President, Vice- President for Operations, Financial Officer, and so on. Running the plates later can identify these individuals. Noting the types of vehicles in the lot can reveal something about the salaries of the employees. A preponderance of luxury or sports cars indicates a high-scale payroll.

Make note of any vehicles with commercial markings for the owning company's insignia or logo. Jot down any license plate numbers. Look for movable assets such as boats, airplanes, recreational vehicles, special equipment such as farm or earth-moving machinery. Write down the commercial markings and license plate numbers of any delivery vans, trucks, or semi-tractor trailers from outside suppliers and vendors. Later, you can contact the traffic department of the trucking companies to get details about the frequency, size, and place of origin of shipments.

If the business has a storage yard, make note of the equipment and supplies kept there. Can you determine what the business manufacturers from the contents of the storage yard? Does the yard look busy? How many forklifts do they have? Where did they purchase them? (Are there dealer markings on the forklifts?) How many trucks are loaded and unloaded in an hour? How many workers are in the yard? Note where the trash bins and scrap bin are. (You may need to visit them later.)

Can you determine what companies supply pallets, shrink wrap, corrugated boxes, and packing materials to the business? Leonard Fuld in *Competitor Intelligence* explains that if an investigator can identify the manufacturer of supplies or corrugated boxes to the target, that supplier can act as an excellent source of intelligence about annual sales. The manufacturer is usually listed on the box. Taking photographs or making notes of this information is a priority on any plant visit. If the operation is primarily an office, then can you discover who supplies the computer paper, stationery, and office items such as paper clips? Pay attention to storage areas, supply rooms, and delivery vehicles for clues. Suppliers and vendors of shipping materials and office items can reveal much about a business.

Waste Disposal and Other Vendors

Do not overlook who handles the waste disposal for the business. Their logo is usually on the trash dumpster. The company servicing the copy machine generally has its label on the machine's side. Vendors providing computer hardware and software support should be duly noted. The company supplying bottled water should not be forgotten, nor the snack machine vendor. Virtually any vendor can provide insight on the size, scope of operations, product lines, and number of employees for a business.

Area Businesses

Make mental note of businesses in the immediate vicinity that may provide services to the target business or its employees. These include restaurants, dry cleaners, office supply outlets, bars, auto repair shops, and so on. They may be worth visiting during peak loads to make employee counts, pick up gossip, and get involved in conversations that lead to productive intelligence on the firm. Owners and operators of these businesses may provide useful information about the numbers of employees. Restaurants and bars nearby may serve as places from which to do limited surveillance.

ADDITIONAL DETAILS

Individual work sites may divulge a great deal about a company's operations. If the business performs contract or construction work at various locations, visiting those sites could reveal the number of employees in the field, the equipment used, and the types of contracts in effect. The main plant site may have little equipment on display. However, going a few miles across town, the investigator may discover the company has an extensive contract to clear land for a park utilizing equipment worth hundreds of thousands of dollars. Checking the local business press for articles about the target may uncover the contracts that they have. The city building department or planning commission may be able to tell you every building permit the target currently has active. The city clerk or the respective city agency should have on file for public inspection any contracts between the city and the target.

If the target is not a construction business, it still may have extensive government contracts. Determine the nature of the business. Then, do an open-record request to relevant state or local agencies. If, for example, it manufactures educational software, it may have a contract with the state education agency or university. Former employees could brief you on the extent of the company's governmental contracts.

The local tax appraisal board is a source on the square footage of the target's plant. This information coupled with estimates on the number of employees and the frequency of deliveries to the site supplies possible insight on the business's sales. Construction dates of expansions at the site, provided by the appraisal board, will suggest the extent of the firm's growth over recent years. Correlating this data with reported sales and financial information from the press, credit reports, or business directories will offer a deep view into the company's finances.

One should not overlook railroad deliveries to the site. Counting boxcars and noting the railroads involved will, over time, produce the names of suppliers and the extent of production at the plant.

Learning to read a site like a hunter would the tracks of a prey is crucial. Count the number of buildings; they indicate the amount of investment in physical plant. Some processes require separate buildings due to safety considerations such as noise, waste products, or dangerous emissions. Handlers of toxic chemicals frequently have to register with the local fire department and secure special permits. These public records will tell you about the size and scope of the manufacturing operation. The federal Occupational Safety and Health Administration (OSHA) may have safety records on the business which are subject to public inspection. State regulatory agencies like the Air Control Board may have extensive permit filings by the target business. Any of these sources can lead to inside financial information about a company's productive capacity, annual sales, and net worth.

Often, an investigator may need the services of an industry expert to interpret the raw data gathered from a plant site inspection. They can tell your client about the target's annual sales, productive capabilities, obsolescence of equipment, and even profitability. For example, the amount of acreage that a building covers may indicate the type of process or assembly going on inside. A "manufacturing" facility where the high percentage of building space goes to office and administrative areas may simply be an assembly operation. Observing heavy commercial carrier traffic at the site will confirm it. The real manufacturing takes place offsite at other facilities or at suppliers' plants. A high ratio of warehouse to production space may indicate the site is just a distribution center.

Checking with the local zoning commission may reveal filings to obtain variances for expansion of physical plant. These filings provide inside information on company ownership in addition to data about the growth of the business. The local municipal utility company may offer as public record the history of power consumption at the site. This data could be another indicator of business growth or decline. Proper maintenance of the site is a sign of business success. If the buildings and equipment visible outside look run down and in need of repair, ask at neighboring businesses how long this decline has been going on. If maintenance crews are evident all over the site, find out what caused the "repair boom."

Are the buildings on the site capable of easy expansion? Or, is their layout locked into a specific mode of operation or production? The size and shape of the buildings may limit the future growth of the business. Current sales may suffer due to limitations in the physical plant. Multistory buildings normally are not readily adaptable to manufacturing processes that require long assembly lines utilizing heavy equipment. The lack of sufficient receiving and loading docks may create bottlenecks in getting materials or product in and out of the plant. A company that has large sales growth touted in the business press but still uses an outdated plant may be a business which cannot raise sufficient capital for expansion.

Leonard Fuld in *Competitor Intelligence* discusses the concept known as an industry's density. If an investigator knows the number of employees and the square footage of the plant's building, they can calculate the Square Feet of Building per Employee. Fuld supplies a table of modern industrial plants classified by product. He states the average Site Size, Plant Size, Land/Building Ratio, Employees per acre, and Square Feet of Building per Employee for each product line. Beer manufacturers have two employees per acre and 1280 sq. ft. of building per employee. The manufacturers of consumer tape recorders employ 30 people per acre and have 239 sq. ft. of building per employee. Obviously, from these figures, the manufacture of beer is more automated than that of consumer tape recorders. Learning to compare your target's statistics with those of industry norms will tell much about its manufacturing and financial strength. A company that remains labor-intensive in an industry which is becoming automated may have serious capitalization problems.

SUMMARY

Nothing can replace careful observation when visiting the target's plant. Key items to look for in the office areas include:

1. Calendars from suppliers and vendors.
2. Business permits or licenses.
3. Address labels on magazines in the waiting room.
4. Nameplates on desks (possible future sources).
5. Annual reports, company newsletters, in-house bulletins in the waiting room.
6. Company's internal phone book by the telephone used by visitors.
7. OSHA and Worker's Compensation Notices posted on the bulletin board.
8. Markings on file cabinets and file folders that indicate the nature of company operations.

Exterior features that need careful observation are:

A. The Neighborhood.
B. Railroad Tracks and Heavy Utility Lines into the Site.
C. Suppliers and Vendors making Deliveries to the Site.
D. Equipment, Vehicles, and Machinery Visible.
E. The Size and Shape of Buildings.
F. The Size of the Parking Lots.
G. Site Security Measures.
H. The Use of Hazardous Materials.
I. Other Businesses in the Vicinity.

After the visual inspection, the investigator must check with local, state, and federal regulatory agencies to uncover permits, zoning variances, and tax rebates applicable to the target company and the site. Local utility companies may also provide information on power, water, and natural gas usage at the site. Use Form 9 to record the plant visit data.

Form 9

The Plant Visit

Case: Date:

Subject: Location:

Neighborhood Setting:

Railroad Service:

Special Utility Lines:

Site Security:

Area Businesses:

Size of Parking Lots:

Size of Storage Yards: Waste Disposal:

Delivery Areas (Size and Type):

Number of Buildings: Their Size and Shape:

Form 9

Continued

Visible Equipment, Vehicles, Machinery:

Vendors, Suppliers, or Customers Identified:

Photographs Taken:

License Plates:

Logos from Delivery Vehicles:

Offsite Sources:

1. Fire Department (Hazardous Materials):

2. Tax Appraisal Board:

3. Utility Companies:

Form 9

Continued

4. City Building Department:

5. Occupational and Safety Administration (OSHA):

6. State Regulatory Agencies:

7. Zoning or Planning Commission:

8. Scans of Local Newspaper Databases:

Chapter 10

ADVANCED SOURCES FOR BUSINESSES

The intensive use of public records carries an investigation probably three-quarters of the way to conclusion. To complete the final
phase, human information is necessary. This chapter presents ideas
for locating the target's suppliers and industry experts who can fill in
the information gaps. In addition, it stresses the importance of proper interviewing techniques.

Describing key business ratios or what trade shows offer serves as
a basic introduction to business intelligence. Some insight concerning
what constitutes valid and reliable sources will complete the examination of intelligence gathering. Hopefully, the reader will learn alternative avenues to discovering business "secrets."

IDENTIFYING THOSE WHO CAN TELL MORE

An investigator can run the license plates of visitors, suppliers, and
vendors, after surveillance of the premises, to get address information
for later contact. UCC filings will provide the names and addresses of
suppliers and creditors. Checking with the editorial staff of the local
business newspaper is another option. If you get stuck and need an
address for a supplier or distributor, *Dun's Million Dollar Directory,
Directories in Print,* or the *Thomas Register of Manufacturers* should do the
trick. Newspaper and periodical indexes such as NEXIS, Business
Periodical Index, Legal Resource Index, and the local newspaper on
CD-ROM should assist in locating:

1. Associates of the Target.
2. Enemies, vocal critics, and watchdog groups interested in your
   Target.
3. Journalists writing about your Target.
4. The Names of Suppliers, Vendors, and Distributors doing business with the Target.

The *Encyclopedia of Associations* and *National Trade and Professional Associations of the United States and Canada* are two reference works which identify professional and trade organizations. Leonard Fuld's *Competitor Intelligence, Directories in Print,* and *Newsletters in Print* provide leads for locating experts. Doing subject searches on the various periodical indexes uncover authors writing about the industry under investigation. Some databases such as Business Periodical Index allow searches by Standard Industrial Classification (SIC) code.

If an investigator cannot find an article about the target's business, they may locate one about a similar business. They can then contact experts at that business who may have insight on the target, and where it stands in the industry as a whole. The directory of manufacturers for your state should list the respective SIC codes for each listed company. Most college libraries will have a directory of SIC codes published by the federal government.

An investigator should not overlook experts within the federal government. Fuld discusses them in *Competitor Intelligence.* Matthew Lesko in his books, *Information USA* and *Info-Power,* deals in-depth with the wide variety of governmental experts available on almost any kind of industry in America. *Info-Power* is now available on CD-ROM which makes searching for the right source that much quicker and efficient.

Directories in Print is an invaluable source in business and financial investigation. When an investigator knows nothing about an industry, this two-volume directory identifies the specific guide or directory that will serve as an information key. For example, in a recent investigation, I needed to know who the Texas distributors were for a manufacturer of coin-operated kiddies' rides. *Directories in Print* identified *Play Meter* magazine's annual directory as a source. I contacted the magazine and they sent their latest directory by U.P.S. for a nominal sum. I found the distributors in the listings.

Other sources for experts include the *Research Centers Directory, Comprehensive Dissertation Index,* and *Books in Print,* all available at the local university library. An investigator should not overlook the resources at the local university's business school. It may have a research department with extensive knowledge about your target business or industry. Such experts can tell you about the norms for an industry. They may explain how the target's business ratios are good or bad in comparison to the industry's norms. Finding an expert with detailed articles or papers written about your target is possible. If a target is in serious financial trouble, an expert may assist in identifying viable parts of the company that could emerge from a Chapter 11 bankruptcy. In complex financial investigations, do not overlook these types of experts.

INTERVIEWING TECHNIQUES

The art of interviewing experts, suppliers, and others concerned with your target involves more than having a prepared list of questions. Being ready to field questions raised by the interviewee is the crux of the art. Investigators should prepare themselves to answer the questions of who they are and why they want the information.

Pretext responses can range from the moderately false, "I'm doing research for a graduate school paper," to the daring, "My company is thinking of doing an acquisition of this business." Whatever pretext you choose, keep in mind that when dealing with a supplier, associate, or vendor of the target, news will probably get back fast. If you feel a pretext is necessary, then use one that is the closest to the truth but is vague enough to be non-threatening. One could truthfully say that he or she was a researcher doing a project for a client that wishes to remain confidential. This company is a representative one selected from the industry that you need more details on. (Just a little embellishment to make them feel comfortable.) If asked about why your client wants the information, tell them that you really do not know; this is one of many routine research projects that you work on. Always try to sound mildly bored; you just have a few routine questions.

Do not ask pointed questions that immediately reveal what you are after. For example, "What are the current liabilities of XYZ Manufacturing?" Do not pose questions which reveal what you already know about the company. "In their last business credit report XYZ showed an account overdue with you by ninety days, is that true?" Leave out the names of individuals in asking your questions. "Has Tom Jonson, XYZ's Treasurer, discussed their accounts receivable problem with you?"

Instead, ask a series of generalized questions which step by step take you to the desired answer. The impression which you wish to create is that your interest is a neutral, scholarly one. For example, you can state: "My research on the industry has revealed that the current ratio for companies like XYZ is 2.3." After some brief comment on this point by the interviewee, you can then ask, "Would XYZ fall into that ball park?" Low pressure, non-direct questioning will elicit most of the information that an investigator needs from a supplier, associate, or vendor.

Obviously, careful planning of the questions beforehand will increase the chances of a successful interview. Special care also is essential to the planning of the when and where of the interview. Telephone interviews are best. With a telephone conversation, creating a pretext is less difficult; having notes spread before you makes asking questions less challenging; you are in comfortable surroundings. Call at times when access to the person in the know is the easiest. This time could be early in the morning or after regular business hours. Both are times when a secretary may not be on duty to screen calls. Officers or executives in a business may be more relaxed and willing to talk.

If the interview must take place face to face, rehearse the meeting in advance. Expect some probing questions and prepare for them. Dress for the part: wearing appropriate clothes for the location. In a formal business office, a suit and a briefcase are a must. In the "blue collar" atmosphere of an automotive parts warehouse, perhaps more casual clothing would be in order. The closer the business's relation to the target, the less advance warning you should give the interviewee. Sometimes going without an appointment places the element of surprise on your side. In any event, keep your visit low-key and friendly. However, avoid becoming the interviewee at all costs. If they just wish to ask you questions without answering yours, politely excuse yourself.

The interviewing of experts is a different matter. Most of the time being completely frank with an expert will assist your investigation. If an expert is seeing you as a courtesy, be respectful of his or her time. Have all research facts organized for quick presentation. Write out your specific questions well in advance. If the expert requires documents or records in advance of the meeting, see that they are sent well beforehand. In cases where the client hires the expert to work with you, write a memorandum to the expert outlining the facts of the case and the specific questions you want addressed. Prior preparation of the expert will give your interview clear focus and save your client case expense.

USING KEY BUSINESS RATIOS

Leonard Fuld lists several sources of business ratios in his book, *Competitor Intelligence.* These ratios allow an investigator to make an educated guess on the financial data of a company based upon known information and industry norms. For example, the Crooked and Corrupt Cement Company has liabilities of about $200,000. Based upon the formula for what accountants call the Current Ratio, you know that the assets divided by the liabilities equals a certain number. By going to the ratio book that covers cement manufacturers, you find that the figure is 2.3. In other words, to find the approximate assets, you multiply $200,000 by 2.3 which yields $460,000.

Investigators will find the necessary reference books such as Dun and Bradstreet's *Selected Key Business Ratios in 125 Lines of Business* in public libraries. Some of the more commonly used ratios are:

1. The Quick Ratio = Cash + Accounts Receivable/Total Current Liabilities.
2. Current Liabilities to Net Worth = Total C.L./Net Worth.
3. Current Liabilities to Inventory = Total C.L./Inventory.
4. Total Liabilities to Net Worth = Total Liabilities/Net Worth.
5. Fixed Assets to Net Worth = Fixed Assets/Net Worth.
6. Current Ratio = Total Current Assets/Total Current Liabilities.
7. Collection Period = (Accounts Receivable/Sales) × 365 days.
8. Inventory Turnover = Sales/Inventory.
9. Assets to Sales = Total Assets/Sales.
10. Accounts Payable to Sales = Accounts Payable/Sales.
11. Return on Sales = Net Profit After Taxes/Sales.
12. Return on Assets = Net Profit after Taxes/Total Assets.
13. Return on Net Worth = Net Profit after Taxes/Net Worth.

Again, the main interest in these accounting tools is not in the ratio alone. Their power to the financial investigator rests in the ability to take one known figure and extrapolate other financial data using the ratio tables. Clearly, if one knows the annual sales and current liabilities for a business, one can deduce reasonable, educated figures on the rest.

While ratios can fill certain gaps in financial information, the investigator must always consider them as just one source of possible data. Remember that the ratios found in the book may not be for a business exactly the same size as your target. Check your results against figures from public records, press accounts, and business databases such as Experian Business Credit and Dun & Bradstreet. In reporting to clients, always identify estimates as such, and cite the sources used in creating any estimate. As a part of preparation for the interviewing process with experts and suppliers, the investigator may wish to develop as many ratios for the target as possible. Keeping these figures available for review by "those who know" will tell one how valid the preliminary estimates really are. If the experts or suppliers concur with your figures, based upon the ratios, then you can report that to your client.

BUSINESS INTELLIGENCE TECHNIQUES

The art of gathering, organizing, representing, and analyzing raw investigative data encompasses the craft of intelligence. This cousin of the investigative process turns information into knowledge. No criminal design or methods are necessary. Rather, the refined tools of interviewing, research, and logic accomplish the desired ends. Logic becomes the crucial factor. How does an investigator know that data gathered is both reliable and valid?

What Constitutes Reliable Data?

High reliability means that a source consistently supplies truthful data that reasonable persons should take heed of. Traditional texts on intelligence gathering discuss a grading scale for rating the reliability of a source. The scale goes something like:

A. Data is random input, no relation to other data.
B. Rare agreement (a 1 in 25 agreement among sources).
C. Data agreement (1 in 10 agree).
D. Almost all sources agree with few exceptions.
E. All sources exactly agree without any exceptions.

While a scale is a useful classification tool, it does not instruct the investigator on how to compare data, nor does it explain where they can find corroborating sources. From the beginning of this essay, we concentrated on the need to correlate information. The theme is that a body of records with their respective individual facts often divulges a hidden, larger truth. We find a nephew in a DWI criminal file who serves as a key officer on several companies. UCC filings disclose a hidden officer in a company. Newspaper accounts provide background on associates, and even enemies, of a target. We can use business credit files to determine debt burdens, cash flow, and assets in a business.

The process follows this order:

1. Start with KNOWN FACTS.
2. Research PUBLIC RECORDS.
3. Do SURVEILLANCE of individuals and premises.
4. INTERVIEW suppliers, customers, associates, and experts.
5. Review NEW FACT SET.
6. Repeat the CYCLE if needed.

The investigator starts with an initial set of known facts which undergo expansion during the first pass of public records. Further development of facts occurs in the surveillance and interviewing phases. An investigator creates a new known fact-set which may receive additional amplifying by repeating the cycle. Only when a financial investigation fails to build by this cyclical method is reliability an issue. If information is reliable, it will lead an investigator to new data. A lack of forward momentum means possibly serious reliability problems.

What Constitutes Valid Data?

Reliable sources may be erroneous. Normally, intelligence analysts use a truth scale to rate the validity of a source:

1. No relationship to reality.
2. Probably untrue (1 chance in 50).
3. Possibly true (1 in 10).
4. Good reason to be true (1 in 3 or 4).
5. Statement exactly describes reality.

The test of validity is in the lateral correlation of data. In other words, the discovery of identical or similar data at FINANCIAL SOURCE 1, NEWSPAPER SOURCE 7, INTERVIEW SOURCE 4, and PUBLIC RECORD 10 increases the probability that this data is true, provided the sources are reliable. The following example may help:

FINANCIAL SOURCE 1: Bank Zero's financial statement from XYZ Company lists annual sales of $100,000.

NEWSPAPER SOURCE 7: An article in the local paper confirms the annual sales figure.

INTERVIEW SOURCE 4: Tom Jackson, a former accounts receivable clerk for the target, confirms the figure.

PUBLIC RECORD 10: A city contract application lists the figure.

The process is much like putting pieces of a puzzle together. Good financial investigators will find themselves going back to the same sources to check facts as they discover new information. For example, learning the name of a new associate from a civil file will prompt the investigator to recheck the local newspaper database, corporate officer records, and so on. This sort of rechecking is quite normal and necessary to successful financial investigation. The greater the number of reliable sources that state something is true, then the greater the chances that it is true. Taking the raw data found in public records through this process, before presenting it to an expert for review, will enhance the quality of that expert's findings.

BACKGROUND ON A BUSINESS

General background on a business or industry comes from several sources. First, periodicals and trade publications provide excellent "inside" data. Locating the right article or publication is not difficult with the following resources:

Business Periodical Index
National Newspaper Index
NEXIS
Newsbank
LEXIS or WESTLAW
Legal Resource Index
OCLC
ABI/INFORM Database
America Online (AOL) or CompuServe: Special Interest Groups
America Online: Newspaper Databases

Most of these indexes and services have been discussed earlier. However, America Online's Newspaper Databases deserve some special note. Imagine being able to search electronically newspapers from other cities. An investigator runs a name in the Chicago paper to gain background information. AOL continues to build this capability. So far, Chicago and San Jose, California are online. Expect more papers in the near future. Even now, the *San Jose Mercury* provides good coverage of the electronic and computer industries with Silicon Valley nearby.

Prodigy, CompuServe, and other Internet gateways provide access to online newspapers around the country Search engines such as Yahoo com are also useful in locating both national and regional newspapers that have online editions

Getting to know local business publications is helpful. For example, the *Austin Business Journal* publishes articles about businesses in my area. A similar publication in your city may provide an index which lists articles about your target. These locally produced periodicals supply coverage of small and medium-sized businesses left out of the national press.

Another source of business background information is FIND/SVP. This New York City research firm offers a wide range of industry and market reports. Their catalog (available by calling 800-346-3787) covers Beverages, Biotechnology, Computers, Drugs, Software, and many other industries. They provide reports on a wide selection of public corporations, and they offer many books useful for business intelligence. Titles include *American Manufacturer's Directory, The Competitive Intelligence Handbook,* State Business Directories for all fifty states, and *Advances in Competitive Intelligence.* Industry reports cover topics such as "The Medical Laboratories Industry," "Food Additives," "Doing Business in Russia," "Latin America: Directory & Sourcebook," and "The U.S. Keyboard Industry." Company profiles include: Abbott Labs, Union Carbide, Nalco Chemical, W.R. Grace, and others. If you need inside information on an industry, this is a good place to check.

Attending trade shows and technical meetings may provide an investigator an unparalleled opportunity to discover detailed information concerning a business. As indicated before, salespeople love to talk about the company that they represent. They will be in abundance at trade shows. Even at technical meetings of professional associations, an investigator will find that members of the technical staff such as engineers, researchers, and technicians will let their "hair down" somewhat. Important information may be less guarded in conversations. One can find listings of times and places for local professional meetings in the business section of the city's newspaper.

As indicated in Chapter 8, another source of financial data is help-wanted advertisements placed in the newspapers. These ads explain expansion plans for a business. They may quote sales figures: "Join a growing $10 million company." Citing assets, such as, "Come work in our $3 million facility," is not uncommon. The ads will also tell about the history of the company and its product lines, "Making quality sporting goods since 1979." Information about the kinds of technical people that they employ will be available. The investigator can learn much about the salary base of the business from carefully reading the job descriptions and salary ranges.

One should not dismiss looking at the local newspapers over the past year or several months. Building an historical perspective on when the company hired certain types of employees will help an investigator understand the business's growth curve. Is it in decline? Or, is it a business to watch? This is excellent information for any experts you located to review for a prognosis on the target.

For a recent overview of the Business Intelligence process, read *Competitive Intelligence* by Larry Kahaner (Simon and Schuster, 1996, available through *www.Amazon.com* and his web site *http://kahaner.com*), and *How to Conduct Business Investigations and Competitive Intelligence Gathering* by Ronald L. Mendell (Thomas Investigative Publications, Inc, 1997, available through ASIS Customer Service at 703-519-6200)

SUMMARY

This chapter explained how to locate suppliers, associates, and vendors of the target. It supplied basic reference sources for finding experts. It gave suggestions for successful interviewing such as keeping inquiries low-key by asking non-direct questions. The text explained the use of key business ratios to calculate unknown financial data. Cross-checking estimates gained from the ratios against public records and expert opinions was also discussed. Finally, the chapter covered utilizing business intelligence techniques to check the validity and reliability of sources. The text explained the methods of Expert Review, Periodical Research, Attending Trade Fairs, and Checking Employment Ads. These methods illustrate the principle of the correlation of data in financial investigation. Use Form 10 for recording interview contacts.

Form 10

Interview Contact

Case: Date:

Subject:

Source:

Method of Contact:

Basis of Knowledge of Target:

Key Assets Identified:

Key Personnel: Annual Sales:

Operations and Locations:

Products and Services:

Cash Flow Data:

Banking Data:

Form 10

Continued

Balance Sheet Data:

Buildings	_____	Mortgages	_____
Plant	_____	Accounts Payable	_____
Vehicles	_____	Loans	_____
Inventory	_____	Tax Liens	_____
Acc. Rec.	_____	Other	_____
Cash	_____		
Real Estate	_____		
Other	_____		

Hidden Assets:

Chapter 11

RECORDING DATA AND
REPORTING TO THE CLIENT

Financial investigation involves the collection of large amounts of raw data. This data must undergo organization and analysis. The client needs the major points of your findings summarized in a clear, concise report. Poor organization or reporting undermines an otherwise good investigative effort. An investigator must see the final work product through the client's eyes. Does the report address the client's primary concerns?

Clients have little interest in "war stories" or in learning about investigative techniques. They do desire to know the "facts" uncovered in the course of the inquiry. More important, they should insist that the investigator explain why the "facts" are true. What is the supporting evidence? Rather than looking upon reporting as a chore, good financial investigators see it as an opportunity to double-check their investigation's rigor. They look for holes in the inquiry: the dead corporation not checked for assets, missed property in a spouse's name, or money hidden in a homestead, not checked for a mortgage paydown. They detect faulty logic and unsupported assertions. An enemy of the target may say the individual has cash "squirreled away" in an out-of-state bank. However, there may be no evidence to support the allegation.

Often, good reporting includes the basis for accepting the reliability and validity of critical information sources. As indicated in the previous chapter, proper correlation of data goes a long way to establish an alleged fact's truth. Citing the supporting evidence for important findings gives your presentation more clout with the client. For example, if one states that John Jones has an undisclosed ownership interest in XYZ Corporation because his ax-brother-in-law says so, that is fine. However, an exceptional investigator does not stop there. One should tell the client that the UCC records and the State Sales Tax records confirm the allegation. If an investigator cannot verify the statement by other sources, the report lets the client know it. Also, adding background information to the report on the reliability of John Jones as source is a definite plus. Be in the habit of placing key pieces of information in a context where the client can make reasonable judgments concerning their value.

If any general rules exist on writing the reports, they are: identify your Sources, and separate fact from opinion. Nothing is more troublesome than to read in a report, "A confidential source states. . . ." Without supporting public sources as backup, the client has nothing by which to gauge this mysterious fountainhead of knowledge. Unless the source can direct your client to documents or other persons which confirm the information, leave it out of the report. Stick to the facts; base any opinions that you have on the facts. Clearly identify any opinion as such, and list your reasons for the opinion. Do not say, "John Jones probably has no assets outside the Austin area," unless you also say, "I base this conclusion on the fact that he has always lived in Austin, holding only minimum wage jobs."

Finally, do not make any statements that are beyond your area of expertise. Do not try to be an accountant or a financial analyst, unless you are one. If your report needs a statement from such an expert, quote directly from your interview notes or attach a copy of the expert's written report.

This chapter explains the basic organization of information during the data-collection phase. It deals with the use of the Universal Public Record Form (see Form 13) and the two summary forms (see Forms 2 and 8). In addition, the text discusses tips and techniques for easier correlation of data through index cards and computer database programs. Continuing with the reorganizing and analyzing of data, the discussion will then explain chronologies, the Association Summary (Form 11), and the Banking Summary (Form 12). Finally, the chapter concludes by illustrating the best methods for writing the Individual and the Business Report for the client.

ORGANIZING DATA

The Universal Public Record Form (UPRF) provides a good tool for recording information found in the records discussed in Chapter 3 and following chapters. Whether it be a UCC filing or a real estate record, the UPRF will serve you well. When you use a form for each record located, the job of summarizing the information on the Individual Asset Summary (see Form 2) will be less confusing and stressful. The data recorded on the Individual Summary then serves as the basis for the Individual Report discussed later in this chapter.

Due to the specialized nature of business records, Chapter 8 introduced several separate data collection forms for doing the business search. The investigator summarizes the information from these forms onto the Business Summary (Form 8). Of course, one uses the UPRF (Form 13) in conjunction with the business search as needed. Depending upon the extent and nature of the investigation, completing summary forms on both the individuals and on the businesses could be necessary.

The use of index cards is an inexpensive, powerful tool to correlate data. Suppose that you are investigating the finances of a Mr. John Jones. In the course of the investigation you note that he owns a 1991 Cadillac with the license plate CROOK1. Surveillance reveals the car parked at more than one address during the evening hours. A Mindy Smith lives at one of those addresses. Mr. Jones lives at one address and owns the property at another. He finances his Cadillac through Bank Zero. Keeping all of these separate bits of information linked to Mr. Jones is a chore. How can index cards help you?

First, one creates a separate card for every person, place, or thing connected with the investigation. The name card "Jones, John" lists things, places, businesses, and persons tied directly to him. Additional cards represent the individual items found on John's card. Other people or businesses have their own cards. The reason why the investigator creates individual item cards is that one thing or person may have multiple connections to other people, places, or things. John's card would contain:

> Owns house at 19887 Maple Street.
> Owns 1991 Cadillac with plate CROOK1.
> Lien on Cadillac with Bank Zero.
> Lives at 5673 San Pedro.

Mindy Smith's card contains the following item of interest:

> Lives at 19887 Maple Street.

Since we already know that John Jones owns the house at 19887 Maple Street, we can deduce a link between Jones and Mindy Smith. The link could be a weak or a strong one. She could just be a tenant of Mr. Jones. But, if we run the plate CROOK1 on the Municipal Court's traffic ticket database, we learn that Mindy Smith has received several moving violations while driving Mr. Jones's Cadillac. This information coupled with the evening sightings at the Smith residence establishes a strong link between the two individuals. One would want to update Mr. Jones's card to reflect this strong link and the same with Ms. Smith's card. The card on the vehicle would show ownership by Jones and regular use by Smith.

If later investigation revealed Smith had a vehicle of her own financed through Bank Zero, one would list her name and vehicle on that card. Then the investigator would pause to reflect: "Is the same bank just a coincidence?" Or, "Did one help the other get a loan?" The index cards provide a flexible, convenient way of perceiving linkages when dealing with a fair amount of data. They offer a discipline to thinking about the significance of a location, person, asset, or thing. One can use the index cards in conjunction with the other forms presented in the book. They are most effective when investigating interlocking companies and officers.

If you find index cards too cumbersome, consider using database programs available for personal computers. The main power of databases rests in their search capabilities. One can ask for all mentions of a 1991 Cadillac in the database. In such searches, linkages will become apparent. An investigator can generate reports which show all the persons linked to a specific person, place, or thing.

Database programs come in two flavors: field-based and freeform. A field-based program requires the user to predefine all the blocks of information utilized in the individual records. One has to tell the program how big and of what kind each field is going to be. After entering all the records, employing a number of different strategies will generate various reports. For example, one could request a printout of all UCC filings involving John Jones between March 1, 1992 and April 1, 1993.

The freeform database allows the user to create separate screens, each under an individual information theme. Within the screen the information is entered in narrative format; fields are not used. For example, the investigator may have a screen under the name "John Jones." Then, that investigator may keep a chronology of what he discovers about Jones: "10-18-92 Observed Jones's 1991 Cadillac at 19887 Maple from 10 p.m. until 1 a.m." Later, the investigator searches the database by any word that appears in the text of any screen. One can search for all mentions of "Cadillac," " 19887," " 1 a.m.," and so on. The freeform database allows for a fluid, loosely structured entering and retrieval of data. What type should you use in financial investigation? The answer depends largely on personal style and the needs of a given case. If one feels comfortable with a structured environment and wants to generate reports from the raw data, then field-based software is the way to go. Otherwise, if entering data in a narrative fashion suits the user, freeform is the answer.

Reorganizing and Analyzing Data

Creating chronologies for business activity can assist an investigator in visualizing connections between businesses, persons, and things. The same technique applies for individuals. People and businesses have analogous life cycles: birth (incorporation), marriage (merger), and death (dissolution). They acquire assets and incur liabilities. Charting a business's activities in a chronology, along with those of targeted individuals, will improve an investigator's understanding of how cash, goods, and decisions flow or evolve over time in the organization under scrutiny.

Sources for chronologies include:

> UCC Filings
> Civil and Criminal Records
> Corporate Records
> Vehicle Records
> Probate Records
> Commercial Databases
> Periodical and Newspaper Accounts
> Biographical Sources

The Jones case's chronology could go like the example below:

> 10-23-92 Jones buys the yacht "Victoria."
> 11-21-92 He marries Mindy Smith.
> 12-11-92 He purchases a home in the Cayman Islands.
> 01-19-93 Jones retires as president of Fly-By-Night Savings and Loan.
> 02-13-93 He moves to Cayman Islands.

03-10-93 Federal regulators shut down Fly-By-Night Savings and Loan.

Chronologies, regardless of their form, help an investigator perceive processes that evolve over time. Individual events, taken by themselves, which reveal little, become most informative when placed in the natural chain of events. Histories teach more than isolated facts. As Richard Saul Wurman argues in *Information Anxiety,* organizing information by time creates new understanding.

The Association Summary

The same sources used for creating chronologies will provide data for an Association Summary (Form 11). This form organizes the names of all associates and relatives discovered during the investigation. Once organized, the names reveal relationships previously not clear.

The Association Summary aims to put on one piece of paper all the associative evidence gathered in the investigation. As the text indicated in Chapter 2, knowing the relatives, associates, and friends of an individual is of immense help in financial inquiries. People place assets in the names of those that they trust. Dead or dissolved corporations serve as hiding places, too. Recording them on this Summary will help prevent them from being overlooked. When references to locations in other cities or states occur in the public record, listing

Form 11

Association Summary

Case: Date:

Subject:

Reference	*Cross-References*	*Reference Date*

them in the Summary insures them being checked later. Just like any other form in this book, the investigator can enter it in a computer file instead of on paper.

An example of an entry on the Association Summary would be: "1991 Cadillac Plate CROOK1" under the heading of Reference with "John Jones buys 2/91" as the Cross-Reference and Reference Date.

The Banking Summary

The Banking Summary (Form 12) draws from the following sources:

> UCC filings
> *Million Dollar Directory* and similar guides
> Motor vehicle liens
> Boat, aircraft liens
> Bankruptcy files
> Court records
> Trash surveillance
> *Martindale-Hubbell* and similar professional directories
> Credit databases

The purpose of this summary is to place the banking information in one central location for easier analysis. This arrangement will aid in placing the financial institutions into link diagrams and charts. Having a quick reference to the banks, credit unions, and loan companies will assist in report writing.

The actual Banking Summary lists the name of the institution, the type of account, the account number (if known), the balance (if known), and the relevant date or dates involved. Under the date field the investigator should also state the source of the data. For example, "UCC" would mean a Uniform Commercial Code filing. One could then list the filing number additionally under the account number field. Two separate dates in the date field represent the original date of the document and when the account balance was last updated, hence the "U" before the date. An investigator can employ similar coding with the account balances; an "H" can mean the highest previous account balance and "C," the current one.

For example, a typical entry line would look like: "Bank Zero" for the Institution with "Auto Loan 123456-789" for the Account and "C

Form 12

Banking Summary

Case: Date:

Subject:

Institution:	Type:	Account #:	Balance:	Date

$12,500 TX Title 2-1-91" for the Balance and Date.

The Banking Summary helps to bring together from dissimilar sources: UCC filings, credit reports, real estate records, vehicle titles, and loan applications, creating a composite banking picture. None of the documents alone tell much; together they say a great deal.

REPORTING ON THE INDIVIDUAL

Use the Individual Asset Summary (see Form 2) as the basis for your report. After extracting the information from the Summary, you may wish to attach a copy of it as an exhibit to the report. Providing copies of the Banking Summary and Association Summary is prudent when reporting on complex cases. The report's goal is to create an overview of the financial condition of the targeted individual. Strive for conciseness in the main body of the report. Emphasize the important points. The attachments can fill in the details.

The outline for the report is as follows:

I. Introduction
   A. Statement of Assignment.
   B. Review of Basic Identifiers (DOB, SSN, Address, etc.).
   C. Target's Occupation and Earnings.

     D. Identification of Spouse and Immediate Relatives.

     E. A Brief One-Paragraph Summary of Your Overall Findings.

  II. Summary of Target's Assets and Liabilities (from Chaps. 3, 5, and 6).

 III. A Discussion of Possible Hidden Assets (from Chap. 7).

     A. Their Location and Estimated Value.

     B. Possible Further Investigative Action.

 IV. The Target's Links to Other Persons.

     A. The Extent of Your Investigation of Other Names.

     B. Further Investigation Suggested.

  V. Target's Business Interests.

     A. The Extent of your Investigation.

     B. Further Investigation Recommended.

 VI. Attachments.

     A. Target's Individual Asset Summary.

     B. Associates' and Relatives' Asset Summaries.

     C. Any Chronologies or Visual exhibits.

     D. Any Banking or Association Summaries.

     E. Relevant Business Summaries.

     F. Crucial Public Documents or Records.

Make it standard practice to include all the major sections of the outline as captions in your report. If the target has no business interests, just state "None" under that caption. This procedure will indicate thoroughness on your part to the client. However, there is no need to attach all the public record forms completed during the investigation. They should be retained in the file for future reference should the client have a question about a specific record.

The report should always state the investigator completed the investigation within the allotted budget. Then, it should further state that certain avenues could be explored with additional funding. For example, if the client initially pays only for a basic asset investigation of an individual and you discover considerable business holdings for that person, no obligation exists beyond the initial identification of those holdings. In other words, to strive for thoroughness to does mean doing work for free.

Always keep the client informed of possible options, but stay within the parameters of the assignment.

THE BUSINESS REPORT

This report can stand alone. Or, an investigator may write it in connection with an Individual Report. The fundamental source document for the Business Report is the Business Summary (see Form 8). The outline for the report is as follows:

I. Introduction
    A. Statement of Assignment.
    B. Links to Individual Reports (if any).
    C. Basic Identifiers on Business.
       (Type, Date Formed, Number of Employees.)
    D. Main Product Lines and Annual Sales.
    E. Brief Overview of Your Findings.
II. Summary of Assets and Liabilities (from Chaps. 8 and 9).
III. Hidden Assets (Especially, Dead or Dissolved Corporations.)
    A. Holdings in Other Businesses. (from Chaps. 7 and 12)
    B. Holdings by Individuals. (see Chaps. 7 and 12)
IV. Analysis of the Business. (from Chap. 10)
    A. Key Business Ratios.
    B. Opinions of Suppliers and Vendors.
    C. Expert Opinions.
    D. Input from Business Press.
    E. Opinions of Enemies, Competitors, and Associates.
    F. Evaluation by Business Intelligence Techniques.
       1. Reliability of Sources.
       2. Validity of Sources.
       3. Checking Special Sources: FIND/SVP, Fuld's *Competitor Intelligence,* special research collections, and governmental sources.
       4. Trade Fairs and Professional Meetings.
    G. Detailed Financial Data.
       1. Cash Flow Analysis.
       2. Balance Sheet Data.
V. Recommendations for Further Investigation.
VI. Attachments.
    A. Targeted Business Summary.
    B. Relevant Individual Summaries.
    C. Any Chronologies or Visual exhibits.

    D. Any Banking or Association Summaries.
    E. Other Relevant Business Summaries.
    F. Crucial Public Documents or Records.
    G. Expert Reports.

Again, as with the Individual Report, there is no need to enter unpaid territory. If the client did not authorize an analysis of the targeted business, then one would skip section IV. In addition, an investigator would not do Individual Reports on the business's officers unless directed by the client. However, the report's section V could suggest future avenues for investigation. When the need of the client requires extensive investigation, the two different types of summaries support the main report well. This portability offers investigators a flexible hand. The main report can be either an Individual or a Business one, depending upon the emphasis the investigator wishes to make. Is the case best explained through people or through the businesses?

SUMMARY

This chapter covered the organizing of data by index cards and by databases. It explained the use of Association and Banking Summaries. It presented chronology tables as tools for analysis. Finally, the chapter concluded by explaining the contents of both the Individual and the Business Report and how each report represents a different emphasis.

As a preview of Chapter 12, we need to return to the book's original theme. The correlation of information among many different sources does wonders. As the investigator understands more, grasping interrelationships between individuals comes quickly. Connections between businesses becomes evident faster. The fictional account that follows demonstrates the correlation technique at work in the preliminary phase of a complex investigation. Pieces of the puzzle come from diverse places: financial and non-financial. The solution goes to the imaginative investigator; one that avoids a rigid mind-set.

Form 13

Universal Public Record Form

Case: Date:

Subject:

Basic Identifying Data

Source: City   County   District   State   Federal   Private   (Circle One)

Agency: _____

Type: Court   License   Criminal Lawsuit   UCC TAX   Real Estate
          Voter   Regulatory   Crisscross or Index   Utility   Newspaper
          Government Pub.   Book   (Circle One)

Document Title: _____   Date:

Media: Database   Print   Microform   CD-ROM   Paper File
            Printout   Electronic   (Circle One)

People Involved

Parties: (1)   _____   Type: _____
           (2)   _____   _____
           (3)   _____   _____

Other Key Names:

Dates and Record Number

Form 13

Continued

Key Dates in Document:

Record or Filing Number:

Description and Notes:

Chapter 12

A FICTIONAL PRELIMINARY INVESTIGATION

John Richards, a private investigator, has a difficult assignment from an attorney representing the family of a deceased construction worker, Fritz Harding. A defective hydraulic jack caused a section of a building to collapse on Mr. Harding. He died within minutes. The manufacturer of the jack was Nepenthe Hi-Press Systems of Austin, Texas. An initial investigation by the family's attorney revealed that Nepenthe was a shell corporation. There were no assets in its name as far as an initial check could determine. Correspondence with the company yielded nothing more than the reply: they did not have liability insurance and were not interested in settling.

A check with the U.S. Patent Office indicated that the design for the jack was not patented and had been in the public domain for many years. Since there was no real property listed in Nepenthe's name in Travis County, Austin, Texas, the company probably used leased manufacturing facilities. From the Texas Secretary of State's office the attorney learned that the President of the firm was Carl Shivers, the V.P. was Karen Shivers, and the Registered Agent was again Carl Shivers. Other than the company being formed in 1979, John had no other facts to begin the investigation.

Financial investigation does not run a linear path. In the following narrative John will return to sources several times as his case knowledge expands. This dynamic aspect of financial inquiries can be frustrating, even overwhelming, to the novice. However, with patience, this recursive approach will develop a rhythm comfortable for the investigator. A greater understanding of how to correlate facts from dissimilar sources will emerge. The investigator will gain an intuition early in the case on how the pieces of the puzzle fit together.

Dull research procedures transform into challenges. One will taste the excitement of the "hunt" in the air.

John realized that Nepenthe Hi-Press Systems' shell was not invulnerable. He could break through the corporate veil by proving the company merely acted as a conduit for funds and assets to other businesses. The primary questions were "Where?" and then "How?"

Knowing where Carl and Karen Shivers transacted business was crucial. Upon establishing their business locations, John could uncover their means of transferring funds. He suspected that Nepenthe was a multi-state operation, involved in more than just manufacturing hydraulic jacks. Their indifference to the client's plight suggested a well-planned multi-corporate structure designed to deflect product liability claims.

Running Nepenthe's name for UCC filings at the Texas Secretary of State produced no records. This result was a strong indicator that the company did business under other names. An Officer/Director search using both of the Shivers's names yielded no additional companies. At this point John realized that he would need a very broad search strategy: a telescope or binoculars to start, not a magnifying glass. Skipping the local courthouse, he ran the three names he had on Business Public Filings and CDB Infotek through an information broker.

Normally, a search would begin locally and spread regionally or nationally as the facts warranted. The logic behind inverting the pattern was to uncover new names and locations. Hopefully, the new leads would eventually bring him back to Austin, Texas and to Nepenthe.

SAN FRANCISCO

CDB Infotek listed Carl Shivers as the president of Jupiter Diversified Investments in San Francisco, California. Jacob Shivers was the vice-president of the company with Karen Shivers as the treasurer. Jupiter was a California corporation established in 1988, two years after Nepenthe. Numerous UCC filings existed for Jupiter in California. Nothing showed up in the all-states search under Nepenthe.

Business Public Filings revealed a judgment against Jupiter for $61,223.86 in San Francisco by Blue Star Leasing Corporation in April 1989. Everything else was negative. With this new initial information, John decided to run some Texas sources to see if he could build anything further locally.

CROSS-TEXAS TRANSPORT

Checking the *Austin American-Statesman* on CD-ROM, John discovered a brief note in the society column about the Shivers. "Karen and Carl Shivers of San Francisco, California attended the M.S. benefit with Janette and Alfred Robertson." Entering the names of the Robertsons on the same database produced a recent business section article on Cross-Texas Transport. The article identified Mr. Robertson as the company's CEO. Providing common carrier service to the southwestern states, Cross-Texas had routes to Louisiana, New Mexico, Arizona, and California. The name Jacob Shivers produced an article profiling the Blue Diamond Copying Service in Austin. Started in 1990, Blue Diamond specialized in doing copywork for local financial institutions. Jacob, originally from California, was the owner of this small business which employs five people.

UCC filings at the Texas Secretary of State revealed that Blue Diamond had a recent loan from Texas Diversified National Bank with five copy machines as collateral. The names on the filing were Carl and Jacob Shivers. The several filings for Cross-Texas listed only Alfred Robertson. Running the Robertsons' names on the UCC database produced no new company names. According to the Texas Secretary of State, the only company where Jacob was an officer was Blue Diamond.

THE MAIN PLAYERS

John made a list for himself of the individuals and companies:

Blue Diamond Copying Service
Blue Star Leasing
Cross-Texas Transport
Jupiter Diversified Investments
Robertson, Alfred
Robertson, Janette
Shivers, Jacob
Shivers, Carl
Shivers, Karen

He decided to do a collateral investigation through a P.I. in California for all the names on the list. Something struck him odd about the two companies both beginning with the word "blue." He also found Carl Shivers's undisclosed interest in Blue Diamond promising. Melissa Sanders in San Francisco would investigate the list through the California Secretary of State for corporate records, California statewide property records, and UCC filings. Meanwhile, John would search civil, criminal, real estate, vehicle, boat, and aircraft records from Texas.

ORGANIZING THE DATA

However, before beginning the searches, John made a labeled manila folder for each name on the list. As he uncovered documents, he would place them in their respective folders. If a document made reference to more than one name on the list, he would make the appropriate number of photocopies so that each affected folder would receive a copy. If new names developed, he created additional folders. Previous experience dictated that good organization from the start would make later analysis easier.

THE KEY PIECE: A PERSONAL BOND

The criminal records in Travis County, Austin, Texas had nothing on any of the individuals. However, in checking the Assumed Name filing for Blue Diamond Copying in the County Clerk's office, John uncovered something curious: the document listed Jacob Shivers as president and Fred Retting as treasurer. Retting's name did not appear as an officer at the Secretary of State's office. John decided to invoke his own rule of thumb: WHENEVER YOU GET A NEW NAME IN AN INVESTIGATION, RUN A CRIMINAL CHECK ON IT. Those files made many connections for him in the past; they had uncovered many hidden links between people. Fred Retting had a DWI in 1989. The bond application in the file revealed Carl Shivers to be Fred's uncle and Jacob his cousin.

BLUE DIAMOND VS. BLUE STAR?

The civil records in Travis County revealed only one lawsuit of interest. Blue Diamond Copying Service had a judgment against Blue Star Leasing, a California corporation, for $60,350 in 1990. After pulling the file, John observed that an agreed judgment had been entered for the amount. In other words, Blue Star had agreed to pay the debt. The Plaintiff's Original Petition alleged that Blue Diamond performed copying work for Blue Star that remained unpaid. It all seemed improbable to John. Why would Blue Diamond be doing copying work for Blue Star in Austin, Texas? And really, would it run to over $60,000?

An "alpha" search of motor vehicles in Texas revealed a 1991 Lexus for Mrs. Robertson, a 1990 BMW for Mr. Robertson, a 1992 Ford Taurus for Jacob Shivers, a 1991 Mercury Sable for Fred Retting, and ten semi-tractor trailer units registered to Cross-Texas Transport. The lienholder for the units was Blue Star Leasing in San Francisco, California. A check of the boat database at the Texas Department of Parks and Wildlife revealed a 60-foot yacht registered to Blue Star Leasing of San Francisco, California. The aircraft database from the Federal Aviation Administration was negative for all names.

INTREPID HOLDINGS

By supplying the business addresses for Cross-Texas Transport and Nepenthe to the Travis County Central Appraisal District, John learned that the owner of these properties was Intrepid Holdings, Inc. of Oklahoma City, Oklahoma. Running Fred Retting's and Intrepid's names at the Texas Secretary of State produced nothing.

However, a call to Oklahoma's Corporate Records yielded information that the president of Intrepid was a Robert Farrell and the V.P. was Fred Retting. The Federal Bankruptcy Court in Austin had only one listing out of all the existing names. Intrepid was a creditor in a bankruptcy filed by Austin Scenic and Artistic Designs, Ltd. in 1992. This Chapter 11 bankruptcy was still active. The principal officer of the business was Mary Retting.

Travis County Appraisal District records showed individual property holdings only to the Robertsons: a homestead valued at $150,000 and one small piece of raw land valued at $37,000.

MELISSA REPORTS

Melissa Sanders in San Francisco called back. The president of Blue Star was Fred Retting, and the V.P. was Mary Retting. Jupiter Diversified Investments rented space in a commercial building. According to the *Directory of U.S. Mail Drops* and a personal visit to the premises, the address for Blue Star was a commercial mail drop. Both companies were in good standing as far as corporate taxes. The only UCC filing was for Jupiter as the debtor and Intrepid as the creditor in April 1992. The listed collateral was office furniture.

A check of property records in the Oklahoma City area revealed that Intrepid leased space in an office building. Land holdings were negative for all of the individuals and businesses. John ran a credit header check on all of the individuals. After getting social security numbers from Voter's Registration, John learned that the Robertsons and the Rettings had listings only in the Austin area. There were several Robert Farrells in the Oklahoma City area, but none of them had adjunct files in other states. With a social security number supplied by Melissa, John discovered an address from 1990 in Galveston, Texas for Carl Shivers. This was the only address for him in addition to the current one in San Francisco. John guessed that if he went to Galveston, he would find the yacht.

INTERLOCKING COMPANIES

This whole setup of interlocking companies served several purposes. First, it provided a means to shift assets and income to lower tax liabilities. Second, keeping the businesses' land poor and having them lease to each other made them lesser targets for lawsuits from creditors and injured parties. And third, through "sweetheart" lawsuits and questionable Chapter 11 actions, they could fend off collection efforts. These practices also made "rearranging" balance sheets easier.

John reasoned that his investigation so far, compared with others, was not that difficult. Normally, questionable business people accomplished the interlocking of companies through middle men or women. They would stick the names of lawyers or accountants in as corporate officers to obscure the true owners. In this case the players felt that their geographic diffusion was sufficient to keep out the light of day. They did not count on Fred Retting's DWI to be the key to understanding.

Since these companies were not investing in real estate, John felt that he had to establish where Nepenthe's income was going. If he could prove that the interlocking companies siphon off Nepenthe's profits, then a lawsuit could attach those assets from the other companies to pay Fritz Harding's family.

John decided to concentrate on financial data. Since these companies were all privately owned, the SEC databases would not be of any help. He did check the microfiche of Dun's Business Identification Service at the public library. From this source he learned two important facts: first, the Dun and Bradstreet identification numbers for each of the businesses, and second, that these businesses had no branch locations. With this information he could do D&B Credit and Experian Credit investigations. Knowing that there were no branch locations made John confident that he had uncovered the basic corporate structures.

ADDITIONAL NEWSPAPER RESEARCH

As an added backup, he ran the names of all the parties on the Business Periodical Index and on NEXIS. John considered these sources to be some of the most powerful intelligence networks at the disposal of a private investigator. The BPI was free at the public library. NEXIS access came through the library of the local newspaper. The online fees were expensive, but the results could often be spectacular. BPI produced an article in a trucking industry magazine on Cross-Texas. In the 1992 profile the company's gross income was estimated at $4.5 million. NEXIS provided two articles from 1991 on Jupiter and Nepenthe.

The Jupiter article was from a San Francisco newspaper which profiled Carl Shivers and "his venture capital investment firm." Jupiter invested heavily in an amusement park associated with the Single Ace

Casino in Las Vegas. A condominium project in Acapulco, Mexico and a limited partnership in Athena United Software of Austin, Texas rounded out their investment portfolio.

A trade newsletter covering the small-tool industry mentioned Nepenthe's "lean operation" in Austin. Using leased space and equipment, Nepenthe imported components from Hong Kong for assembly into several different types of industrial hydraulic jacks. The article estimated annual gross sales of $5.6 million. Given Nepenthe's low overhead, the profile considered the company to be in a competitive position for the foreseeable future.

John made note of the article's author, Richard Carel, and located an address for the publication out of *Newsletters in Print*. He would follow up with Richard later regarding the sources he used for the article.

BUSINESS CREDIT SOURCES

Concentrating the D&B and Experian credit searches on just Jupiter, Nepenthe, Intrepid, and Athena, John played an educated hunch that these were the major cash centers. This tactic not only reduced case expense, but it also avoided a common pitfall: information overload. Financial investigations of interlocking businesses can produce too many names and leads too quickly, if not managed adroitly. Proper management meant following your intuition. Ninety-five percent of the job involved discovering the overall corporate and financial structure. Playing one's hunches would take an investigator to this desired overview nine times out of ten. Experience taught John to avoid endless "rabbit trails" by this method.

D&B and Experian credit databases provide a summary of credit transactions by a business with other businesses. The databases rate these transactions (loans and purchases on credit), called trades, by several factors:

1. The High Credit. (The highest past balance on the account.)
2. Account Balance. (Current balance on the account, sometimes called the Low Balance.)
3. Current Status. (Percentage of account balance not past due.)
4. Days Beyond Term. (Percentage of account balance past due by time category: 1-30 days, 31-60 days, 61-90 days, and over 90 days.)

Business credit information offers insight into the financial interaction between companies. It identifies suppliers and vendors. It can also tell you about the cash flow of the targeted business and what kind of current debt burden it faces. Unlike consumer credit information, anyone with the desire to pay the charges may have access to the databases. (Rather than set up his own accounts with D&B or Experian, John used the services of an information broker.)

The credit record on Nepenthe was enlightening. In the past twelve months it had six active trade lines. Four of them were with East-West Trading Partners, Ltd. of San Francisco, California. The highest credit extended was $165,000; the lowest was $89,785. The breakdown was $165,000 (high)/$79,000 (low), $89,700/$23,000, $97,000/$15,000, and $106,000/$28,000. The payment trend of the company was that it paid bills within sixty days. It was current on terms. The Public Record section of the report listed no civil suits or judgments. Cross-Texas Transport made up the remaining two trade lines with a high credit of $38,954 and a low credit of $15,674. None of the current accounts showed past due or days beyond terms. The non-active accounts with zero balances consisted of two 1992 entries showing loans of $350,000 and $400,000 paid off to Jupiter Diversified Investments.

All of this made sense to John. The actual business operations and decisions of Nepenthe took place in San Francisco where the company's Hong Kong trading partners were. They located the plant in Austin, Texas to take advantage of lower wages and taxes. Also, Cross-Texas Transport provided transportation services for the company and acted as a local conduit for cash. Athena United Software was also conveniently nearby. The loans to Jupiter were actually cash transfers. Nepenthe was not a part of the sham lawsuits because the owners did not want its credit record clouded. Such a cloud could interfere with lines of trading credit from Hong Kong.

ATHENA UNITED SOFTWARE

Athena United Software had one trade for the last twelve months. The current balance was zero, and the high credit was $135,000. The creditor was Jupiter Diversified Investments. John checked the *Austin American-Statesman* CD-ROM database for stories on Athena. An article in the business section of the July 18, 1992 issue indicated that the company had contracts with the Texas Department of Commerce to manufacture an electronic directory of Texas businesses. Corporation records at the Secretary of State revealed Richard Derwin to be the company's president and registered agent. *The Texas Legal Directory* listed Derwin as a partner in Scott and Derwin, an Austin-based law firm specializing in corporate and commercial law. Was Athena being fronted by Derwin? If so, it was an exception to the rule for the way the other companies operated.

Shivers's Hidden Interest

John answered the question by doing an Open Records Act request to the Texas Department of Commerce. The contract documents revealed that the signatures for Athena were Richard Derwin, President and Carl Shivers, Vice-President. Athena was the exception to the rule, because the Shivers family did not want their name appearing on too many easily accessible Austin public records. Carl remained the undisclosed officer in the corporation. Athena was another profit center for the Shivers's network of companies. Even though it was in Austin, too, tying Athena to Nepenthe was not possible without this considerable investigative effort.

JUPITER'S CREDIT REPORT

Jupiter had three active trades in the last twelve months with East-West Trading Partners, Ltd. with high credits of $135,232, $23,856, and $18,000. The current balances were $28,787, $5000, and $9500. Intrepid showed one trade with Jupiter as the creditor with a high credit of $134,000 and a current balance of zero. This data further confirmed that Jupiter was the nexus of Shivers's financial system. When warranted in later court action, Harding's lawyer could subpoena the loan and account records of East-West Trading Partners, Ltd. and those of the other interlocking companies. Coupled with the Texas Department of Commerce contracts, these financial records could go a long way to pierce the corporate veil.

BANKING INFORMATION

In addition, D&B and Experian reports also provided useful banking information on the targeted companies. Jupiter's bank is First United of San Francisco. The same holds for Intrepid and Nepenthe. Athena has its accounts at Bank One in Austin.

Now that he had the basic structure in place, John decided to check on Blue Star Leasing, Cross-Texas Transport, Blue Diamond Copying Service, and Mary Retting's Austin Scenic and Artistic Designs. None of the trade information from business credit suggested anything other than Jupiter was the linchpin. All of the other Austin-based businesses also have their accounts at Bank One. Blue Star was at First United. Again, John thought that a subpoena to the respective banks would uncover much about the sham corporations.

To complete the scanning phase for information, John consulted several remaining print and electronic sources. He used the *Encyclopedia of Associations, Directories in Print,* and *Newsletters in Print* to learn the names and addresses of the San Francisco Hong Trade Association and the National Construction Tool Society. These organizations could provide valuable business intelligence information later in the investigation. Keeping in mind that the income estimates for the companies needed further documenting, John reasoned industry experts could provide the needed data.

LEGAL RESOURCE INDEX

At the University of Texas library, John ran all the business names on Legal Resource Index. Surprisingly, only the name of Single Ace Casino turned a hit, the reference was from a *New York Times* article of January 13, 1993. The article dealt with numerous personal injury lawsuits filed against Las Vegas casinos by customers injured on the premises. In reading the article off of the library's microfiche, John learned that the Single Ace was among a growing list of casinos that tried to protect themselves through the legal device of a limited partnership.

Relating the ordeals of plaintiff attorney, Charles Rasper, the article outlined the difficulties of litigating against the casinos. John made note of both the attorney and Ken Austin, the author of the article. They could be good sources of information about Single Ace and the Shivers's organization.

Checking on WESTLAW online through the client attorney's office revealed no appellate cases on any of the businesses. Even with the litigation against Single Ace, nothing went beyond the trial court level yet. At his personal computer he signed onto America Online to gain access to the *San Jose Mercury News* database to see if he could pick up any recent news stories about the San Francisco companies. Nothing new turned up. He also checked the *PC World* magazine database to see if there were any stories about Athena United Software. Again the answer was zip. Since computer services like America Online have bulletin boards for special-interest groups (SIGs), he decided to post a message on the Business Software SIG for anyone with background information on Athena.

John also referred to the *Directory of Texas Manufacturers* and Dun's Financial Records Plus on DIALOG to see if he overlooked any facts about the various businesses. The *DTM* indicated that Athena has twelve employees and Nepenthe has thirty. Both companies have single business locations in Austin. The officers listed for the companies were those found in the public record. The standard industrial codes (SIC) were for the manufacturers of software and construction tools respectively. In other words, the data fell in line with what John found from other sources.

BUSINESS RATIOS

In accessing DIALOG's Dun's Financial Records Plus (FRP), he found business ratios for Nepenthe. Business ratios are methods for the quick testing of a business's financial health. John set them aside for analysis later in his investigation. He planned to plug into the formulas some of the financial figures he got off the NEXIS articles and from the Experian and D&B databases. Then he could compare them with the figures off of Dun's FRP. Dun's also supplied some balance sheet and income statement data. John had a printout made for analysis later by an accountant who would act as an expert before the court on the sham corporations. The plaintiff's attorney would need that type of technical assistance due to the complexity of the interlocking companies. A good financial investigator does not shy away from involving an accountant when trying to pierce an elaborate corporate veil. John realized long ago that his role in these types of cases was to gather evidence for expert analysis. He knew better than trying to be an accountant.

BIOGRAPHICAL BACKGROUND

John also consulted *Biography and Genealogy Master Index* published by Gale Research. While he did not find an entry on Carl Shivers, he did discover one on his father, James Shivers. In checking the cited biographical work, John learned that Mr. Shivers was a prominent Beaumont, Texas businessman who founded the Third Coast Toolworks in 1963. He later acquired the Criterion Corporation and merged Third Coast with it in 1983. James Shivers died in 1984. A subsequent check at the Texas Secretary of State's corporate records revealed dissolution of Criterion in 1986. John made note to run Criterion's name in a renewed asset check at the advanced level.

SUMMARY

The greatest tools at work for a financial investigator are imagination and suspicion. Where an accountant may become essential in an investigation, the investigator must recognize that their inquisitive skills get the necessary data for the accountant's analysis. While accountants frequently stop at the figures, investigators look for the motives behind the figures.

Like John, the financial investigator must uncover in the preliminary phase:

1. Financial data about the involved businesses.
2. A list of involved persons.
3. A list of involved companies.
4. A list of organizations and experts who can tell more.
5. A list of reporters, enemies, and informants who know more about the businesses and persons involved.

The next step may involve analyzing the initial data using some of the tools found in Chapter 10. The Banking and Association Summaries would be most helpful in this case. Link analysis would uncover the power relationships in the Shivers's family of interlocking businesses. A chronological table would assist in understanding the evolution of the shell businesses.

Chapter 13

INVESTIGATING USING THE INTERNET
AND OTHER SOURCES

Mary Jackson wants to divorce her husband of eight years' Peter Jackson, whose sexual infidelities have become unbearable. Unfortunately, the disparity in their financial resources leaves Mary at a great disadvantage. Not having worked outside the home since the inception of their marriage, Mary relied on Peter to pay the bills and finance her life. Her knowledge of their monetary power ends at the property line of their $1.2 million home. Other than her 1998 Lexus and Peter's 1999 Land Rover, she lacks insight into what else they own and owe.

With some funds available from a household checking account, she retains a family law attorney for some advice. The attorney counsels Mary to educate herself about her husband's financial affairs. Somewhat embarrassed, she only knows that Peter is a vice president at a computer company, so she agrees to learn what she can. At the attorney's suggestion, Mary consults with an investigator, Richard Denison, who specializes in asset investigations.

Richard agrees to give her a shopping list of needed information. He outlines a plan where Mary will feed him facts that will serve as the basis for online research. Richard hopes that he can develop a profile using electronic resources saving his client both time and money.

He provides the following checklist for Mary:

1. Basic identifiers on husband (see Chapter 1).
2. The names and business locations of all corporations or businesses in which the husband is an officer or owns an interest.
3. A list of any known stocks, mutual funds, or bond holdings.
4. Insurance policies currently active.
5. Any financial statements for the husband for the last three years.
6. A list of all credit card accounts.
7. Income tax returns for the last three years (with W-2's and 1099's).
8. Canceled checks, check registers, and bank statements for the

last three years.

9. A list of real estate owned

10. Vehicles, boats, and aircraft owned.

11. Copies of calendars and appointment books for the last twelve months.

12. Copies of all active leases, documents pertaining to sales or purchases of assets, and the sales or purchases of business or investment interests.

13. A list of any valuable collections such as stamps, coins, artworks, and so on.

GENERAL INSTRUCTIONS FOR MARY

Richard counsels Mary that she will have to learn to be a detective. When her husband is not around, she can poke into his files. Basic identifiers are available on income tax records, mutual fund statements, and on bank loan applications. And, of course, Peter's wallet is frequently lying on his desk in the study or on the bureau in the bedroom.

He tells Mary that when looking through Peter's files make notes of the names of any corporations, partnerships, or limited partnerships she sees on the file tabs. If possible, try to discover from the file contents the state where the business is incorporated or registered.

She can glean from stock certificates, bonds, mutual fund statements, and brokerage statements the extent of Peter's holdings. Noting the number of shares for each security is, of course, critical.

By reading each insurance policy's declarations page, she can list the name of each insurance company, the policy number, the amount of coverage, any beneficiaries, and the type of coverage (life, casualty, or property).

Financial statements detail the assets, liabilities, and net worth of an individual of a business. She should look for file tabs like "Financial Statement–Jackson, L.P." Bank loan applications may also contain financial statements, so she should look for folders pertaining to commercial or personal loans.

Credit card statements, check registers, bank statements, and canceled checks speak to the destination of funds when a witness otherwise desires silence on the issue. They act as invaluable guides on the tracing of funds. Richard counsels Mary to copy all these bank records that she can for the last three years. She should strive, however, to keep items in chronological order, especially retaining checks with their respective bank statements.

Income tax returns and their accompanying documents like W-2's and 1099's detail not only what a person or business earns but what deductions they take. Those deductions and write-offs may reveal previously unknown holdings.

Deeds of trust, warranty deeds, releases of liens, tax appraisal statements, and tax bills for real property all serve to identify owned real estate. Financial statements may also contain a schedule of owned real property along with any mortgage debt figures. And, of course, mortgage payment books also act as pathfinders for locating real estate. In composing a list of real estate, Richard stresses with Mary the importance of stating the street location of the property and its legal description. Detailing any tax appraisal district parcel numbers for the property and the name and address of the mortgage holder is also very helpful.

Mary will look for folders that contain titles or registration documents for vehicles, boats, trucks, and aircraft. Insurance policies on the above will also have identifying information. Loan payment books serve as pointers, too. In compiling a list, writing down the VIN (vehicle identification number), if applicable, the hull identification number, a brief description of the vehicle, boat, or aircraft, and any registration numbers (along with the state or agency of registration) goes a long way to researching these assets successfully.

Calendars and appointment books identify when transactions or "deals" took place. They also identify business associates, interests, and relatives (see Chapter 2).

Documents pertaining to leases and the sales or purchases of business assets reveal income and expenses that may not be found in a financial statement. An income producing property may be recently acquired and not yet listed. Or, a new debt or expense regarding an asset may be something left off of a financial statement for various reasons. Since the arrangements reflected in these documents may be complex, copying them for analysis later is usually the best policy.

Mary tells Richard that Peter has an extensive coin collection that she has seen only glimpses of over the years. Peter keeps it in their safe deposit box. Mary does remember signing the joint tenancy agreement on the box several years ago. She can probably find the key.

Richard recommends that Mary first try to find an index or a catalogue of the coin collection compiled by Peter. That list will save Mary many hours in trying to catalogue the collection. But, in any event, Mary will want to examine the contents of the safe deposit box at some point. Richard suggests that she examine the safe deposit box last. That way, if Peter gets suspicious about the safe deposit box entry, all of her other research will already be done.

Prior to entering the box, Mary should have a relative that she trusts send her by registered mail some document on the family history deemed valuable or "treasured." That document should remain unopened in its envelope. When she examines the box's contents, she can place the envelope right on top of everything inside the box. When Peter sees Mary's signature on the entry card for the box, she has a plausible reason for entering the box. She just says, "Aunt Rosie sent me my great-great-grandfather's confederate soldier's pension documents for safekeeping. I just threw the envelope in the box." The fact the envelope remains unopened lends credence to the cover story.

If Mary needs to catalogue the coin collection from scratch, she should obtain a book on coin values prior to going to the box. After familiarizing herself with the book she can take it with her along with pens and paper in a briefcase into the examination room at the bank.

CORPORATIONS AND BUSINESSES

In her research of Peter's files, Mary found only one affiliated corporation. Peter serves as a director in Sterling Products, Inc. located in Amarillo, Texas. Richard ran the company's name on web search engines like yahoo.com and altavista.com. He found Sterling's web site that revealed the company sells retail on the Internet various southwestern jewelry items for men. So, Peter is trying a line of business outside of his day job. Richard's experience taught him that when an executive in a high-tech company runs a small-scale, low-tech business on the side, he usually is seeking a diversion. He's not trying to build a business empire.

Just to be safe, Richard looks up the telephone number for the Texas Secretary of State (SOS) from the *Investigator's Little Black Book 2* by Robert Scott. By calling the Texas SOS, Richard learns how to gain online proprietary access to their database. From the database Richard can run Peter's name to find out if he has other companies where he serves as an officer or director in Texas. As he suspected, Richard does not find any other companies.

A nationwide search under executive name is also possible through CDB Infotek (*www.cdb.com*), a proprietary database provider. Their telephone number is 800-892-7889. In addition to their Business Directory database, CDB provides locating services on corporations and limited partnerships, UCC filings, bankruptcies, liens, and judgments. Again, a nationwide search under Peter's name does not yield any other companies.

Merlin Information Services at *www.merlindata.com* offers access to national bankruptcies, new business filings nationwide, and corporate records from Texas and many other states. In addition to web access, their toll free number 800-367-6646 enables investigators to order CD-ROMs containing information from the databases of many states. Ranging in content from UCC filings in California to corporate records in Texas, specific requests occurring regularly in the same jurisdiction can be had from CD-ROMs at a reasonable cost.

OPEN (Online Professional Electronic Network) whose web site is *www.openonline.com* and whose telephone number is 800-935-OPEN offers similar corporate locating services. In checking Merlin and OPEN, Richard still has no additional businesses developed for Peter. So, he feels fairly confident that avenue is a dead end.

From Dun and Bradstreet's web site, *www.dnb.com*, Richard obtains a Business Information Report on Sterling Products. The report confirms no affiliates or subsidiaries for the company. Since the business started only two years ago, the report has no financial statements and a modest payment history with a high credit of $5,000 from a jewelry wholesaler. The two officers listed for the business are Peter D. Jackson and Carl Jaspers. Neither of them has biographical information on file.

Since Peter Jackson is not an uncommon name, knowing his middle initial helps to weed out similar but false matches on nationwide database searches. Also having the subject's history, where he lived and worked before, helps in the process of eliminating questionable matches. In Peter's case, Mary indicated his activities were confined, for the most part, to Texas. So, Richard was able to ignore a Peter

Jackson, the president of a company in Idaho.

For companies that are publicly traded, the Security and Exchange Commission's Edgar database, available on the web at *www.sec.gov/edgarhp.htm*, offers extensive financial data and biographical information. Persons suspected of owning major blocks of stock (more than 5%) are listed on SEC Online which is available on CD-ROM at major libraries.

In profiling public companies and larger private businesses, the following web sites are useful:

1. CNN Financial Network (*www.cnnfn.com*).
2. PR Newswire (*www.prnewswire.com*).
3. Quicken (*www.quicken.com/investments/snapshot/*).
4. Creditworthy.com (*www.creditworthy.com*)
5. Yahoo.com ("Yahoo Finance" *www.yahoo.com*)

If a targeted individual is an officer or director in a charitable organization, information about the charity is available through the web. First, to find out if a charity has IRS recognition, run the name at *www.irs.ustreas.gov/plain/tax_stats/soil/ex_imf.html.* Second, *The Investigator's Little Black Book 2,* which is, by the way, an excellent reference resource for financial investigations, recommends requesting a hardcopy of the non-profit organization's tax return by Form 4506A. You can download the form off the web at *www.irs.ustreas.gov/ forms_pubs/forms.html.* Another good site for information is the National Charities Information Bureau (NCIB) at *www.give.org.*

STOCKS, BONDS, AND MUTUAL FUNDS

Obviously, nothing on the web will tell what is in the stock portfolio of a given individual. However, the web is an invaluable tool in determining the current market values of stocks, bonds, or mutual funds. The web also provides excellent background information on companies and various investment instruments and securities. Good sources on the web for investment information include:

1. *Yahoo.com* (Finance section).
2. Edgar (SEC).
3. AOL web interface (Use the search feature).
4. *Snap.com.*

Any of these services will allow searching by the company's name. Often, a simple search by name will reveal the company's ticker symbol. From the ticker symbol, you can learn the current market value. Many services like snap.com and AOL.com will allow you to set up monitoring on a stock, mutual fund, or bond so you can track its value automatically.

Richard learned from Mary's list that Peter had the following securities:

Union Oil	350 shares
California Development	100 shares
Microsoft	700 shares
Dell Computers	180 shares

From a few minutes of online research, Richard placed a dollar value on each block of stocks. He also did basic research on Union Oil and California Development and learned they were both stable securities with good track records.

INSURANCE

Unless an insurance policy has cash value, it remains only a contingent asset. Some loss has to occur for it to have value as a liquid asset. The main purpose then in checking out insurance policies is to make sure the insurance company writing the policy is sound financially. An excellent source for obtaining financial ratings of insurance companies is A.M. Best. A.M. Best's web site at *www.ambest.com* provides ratings on about 6,000 insurance companies. It also has excellent links to insurance regulators, adjusters, agents, and affiliated businesses in the insurance field. The site is a major gateway to obtaining background information on almost any American insurance company.

In evaluating a target's insurance policy, follow these steps:

1. Determine the type of policy: life, casualty, or property?
2. Read the declarations page to establish the face amounts of coverage.
3. Identify who is insured and who the beneficiaries are from the declarations page or the attached application.
4. Check the dates of coverage to make sure that the policy is still in effect. If the policy is a life or an annuity where premiums

get paid monthly or quarterly, verify from bank statements or check registers that the premiums are current.

5. If a life or annuity policy, look for a schedule in the policy language that explains how cash value accumulates and what interest rate accrues. The web site may give current interest rates paid on cash values.

6. Make note of the agent who sold the policy and now services the account. You may be able to call the agent to obtain additional information about the policy's surrender value and coverages.

7. Check out the financial stability of the insurance through A.M. Best's site.

Richard reviewed the policies Mary found in Peter's papers. Those covering the home and the automobiles were all standard casualty policies written by well-known, stable insurance companies. Peter's life insurance policies were:

1. Transamerica for $500,000 payable to Mary.
2. Midwest Life for $300,000 also payable to Mary.
3. California Life for $300,000 payable to Marina Del Rey Interests, L.P.

The last life policy puzzled Mary; she had never heard of Marina Del Rey Interests, L.P. Based upon the business name, Richard believed it to be a limited partnership that Peter owns shares in. Judging from the size of the insurance policy, Richard reasoned that Peter probably has a general partner's share rather than that of a limited partner. He would have to investigate this lead further.

The only other surprise was a hull and liability policy issued by a California Marine Insurance Company on a 26-foot Sea Wonder sailboat. Mary was a bit stunned by this policy because she had never been on any boat owned by Peter during their marriage. She didn't have any idea where he kept the boat. Richard felt a good guess for the boat's location would of course be Marina Del Rey, California, but again he had another avenue to pursue. In checking California Marine on A.M. Best's site, he noted that the company had a good financial rating.

FINANCIAL STATEMENTS

Keys to finding assets, financial statements, which the subject thought no one else would see but the bank, reveal stocks, bonds, bank accounts, real estate holdings, ownership in businesses and income producing properties, and even collectibles previously unknown. Often they contain account numbers or the location of real property. Indeed, financial statements are a roadmap, a lantern to the financial investigator.

Look for them with bank loan documents, real estate mortgage applications, and with business plan proposals. Sometimes, an adversary who has received a "raw deal" from the subject may be willing to share the target's financial statement. And certainly, a properly trained spouse, like Mary, trying to obtain their "freedom" can keep an eye out for them amid the sea of a target's documents.

Fortunately, the financial statement Mary found for Peter was quite recent. Most of it covered known territory; however, in addition to Marina Del Rey Interests, L.P., the statement listed as business interests a Tri-State, L.P. and Dominion Computing, Ltd. of Montreal, Canada along with the known Sterling Products, Inc. in Amarillo, Texas.

Foreign businesses are becoming easier to profile and to obtain details on their operations, thanks to the Internet. Using web search engines such as *altavista.com*, *yahoo.com*, and *snap.com*, an investigator can first find what's really available on web sites. And employing a resource like *www.deja.com* (also known as *www.dejanews.com*), an investigator may locate information about a foreign company in newsgroups.

Newsgroups exist on almost every conceivable subject; some of the ones used by investigators in, say skiptracing, include *alt.binaries.missing-adults*, *alt.crime*, *alt.missing-adults*. Those useful in researching foreign businesses and business practices include: *soc.culture.australian*, *soc.culture.canada*, *soc.culture.mexican*, and so on.

An investigator should not overlook Dun and Bradstreet (*www.dnb.com*) as a resource for business information. Normally, their coverage of Canada, Mexico, Australia, Japan, Europe should meet most needs. Additionally, Infomart Online at 800-668-9215 and Control Data Systems Canada Ltd. at 613-723-1174 have coverage on Canadian businesses and corporations. Gaslamp Quarter

Investigations in San Diego, California at 619-239-6991 and Pan American Investigations in Tucson, Arizona at 520-297-9318 also have extensive contacts for finding information on Mexican businesses and on gathering business intelligence "south of the border."

In the case of Dominion Computing, Ltd., Richard discovered through running a Dun and Bradstreet report online that Peter was not listed as an officer or director. The $70,000 listed as his interest was probably just common stock. In checking on the New York Stock Exchange (NYSE) via the Internet, Richard learned Dominion traded on the NYSE as American Depository Receipts (ADRs) at about $71 per share. The company has a good rating from analysts (as per *www.cnnfn.com*) as a major wholesaler of computer equipment in Canada and Europe.

Tri-State, L.P., however, still remained a mystery.

CREDIT CARDS

Credit card charges on Peter's accounts were largely for consumer goods and restaurant expenses that Mary was aware of. Yet, two items did stand out. First, a monthly charge of $325 for membership and boat slip fees appeared for the Marina Del Rey Resort and Yacht Club. To Richard it was clear now where the sailboat was moored. And second, a recent hotel charge in Phenix City, Alabama also caught Richard's eye. Could it be that Tri-State, L.P. was registered in Alabama? He had done an "all state" scan on several databases for Tri-State, L.P. and found nothing.

With the clue from the credit card statement, he decided to check with the Secretary of State (SOS) in Alabama through *www.sos.state.al.us/business/corporat.htm*. While Alabama's web site didn't currently support online searches of the corporate database, Richard was able to locate a telephone number for the SOS. So he gave them a call. Tri-State, L.P. turned out to be ALA Tri-State, L.P. with Carl Jaspers as the general partner. Credit card statements, even though they normally represent debts, provide paper trails to assets that you may not know about or for which you have incomplete or incorrect data.

INCOME TAX RETURNS

In Peter's case, his tax returns filled in details where Mary's knowledge was incomplete or at best rudimentary. Peter works for Prometheus Intelligence Systems as Senior Vice President of Operations. He earns $620,000 per year of which about $320,000 is performance bonuses.

The returns also contained supplemental forms verifying that Marina Del Rey Interests, L.P. and ALA Tri-State, L.P. are ongoing, active limited partnerships. Last year's income from Marina Del Rey was $7,834 and from ALA Tri-State $4,396. Sterling Products was little more than a hobby with a net income of only $1,100.

Mary knew nothing of the limited partnerships. Seeing only enough of the 1040 each year to affix her signature, Peter never showed her any of the attached schedules. She didn't think to ask about them. Now embarrassed by all that and the fact she didn't know the exact name of where Peter worked: "Prometheus something," she felt her education was long overdue.

An income tax return provides a great deal of essential data:

1. Where the subject works, including, their job title. With the correct company name, an investigator can search for a web site. The web site may contain useful information about executive compensation, pension plans, 401(k) plans, stock options, and bonuses.
2. Interest income.
3. Dividend income.
4. Details about businesses and partnerships.
5. Income-producing property owned.
6. Royalties.
7. Salary income.
8. Social Security number.

In Peter's case, the web site for Prometheus did confirm a generous 401(k) plan for all employees. Unfortunately, Mary could not find any records for the plan in Peter's files. Richard theorized that Peter might have those records at his workplace office along with any stock or stock options pertaining to Prometheus. He would highlight this theory as a possible lead for Mary's attorney to pursue in legal discovery once a lawsuit for divorce commenced.

BANK STATEMENTS AND CHECKS

Two interesting items surfaced in reviewing the bank statements, checks, and check registers. Over a period of two years, Peter wrote checks to ALA Tri-State totaling $65,000. The backsides of the checks showed processing by First Trust in Phenix City, Alabama.

And, over the same period, checks totaling to $7,500 were payable to Thomas Jefferson Life Insurance Company in Nashville, Tennessee. A memo notation on the face of the was "Sandra Johnson-PA173679." Richard located a web site for Thomas Jefferson Life. From the site's content, he found the name of a local agent. He made a telephone call to the agent to clarify what kind of a policy PA173679 represented. The agent commented that all policies beginning with "PA" were annuities. That particular policy in the series commencing with "17" allowed the owner to contribute funds until age sixty-five (65).

At first, Mary did not recognize the name, Sandra Johnson. However, she long suspected a Beverly Johnson of being a paramour of Peter's. Mary recalled now that Beverly has a daughter, Sandra, who is three years old. Both shock and disgust broadcast from Mary's face when she realized the implications of the annuity. Richard, while sympathetic to Mary's feelings, told her it was an avenue that warranted further investigation before any final conclusions could be made.

REAL ESTATE

Richard used several sources to check real property holdings for Peter in both Texas and California, the states where Peter had the most activity. When only the homestead owned jointly with Mary turned up in Texas, Richard also checked Alabama that unfortunately also was negative. The sources included:

1. Experian (formerly TRW REDI) at *www.experian.com*, telephone number 800-421-1052.
2. CDB Infotek's Real Estate databases.
3. Merlin's California Statewide Property database on CD-ROMs.

It appears that Peter's favorite investment vehicle is the limited partnership and not real estate.

VEHICLES, BOATS, AIRCRAFT

An "alpha search" under Peter's name in Texas did not reveal any additional vehicles for him. A similar check in Alabama was also negative. Using Merlin's People Finder and CDB Infotek for California, no hits came up for vehicles for Peter. The only match was the sailboat at 1137 Wharf Drive in Marina Del Rey registered under the name Peter D. Jackson. A check of the FAA's database revealed no aircraft registered to Peter.

Sources used by Richard included:

1. For Texas watercraft, the Texas Parks and Wildlife web site is *www.tpwd.state.tx.us/boat/boat.htm*. Their telephone number is 512-389-4828.
2. The U.S. Coast Guard's database's telephone number is 202-267-0780.
3. In California, the licensing body for boats is the Department of Boating and Waterways (DBW) at *www.ca.gov/* with a telephone numbers of 888-326-2822 and 916-263-4326. The DBW showed no lienholder on the sailboat.
4. For values on watercraft and boats, Richard checked the N.A.D.A. Marine Appraisal Guide from N.A.D.A. Appraisal Guides at *www.nadaguides.com*, telephone 800-966-6232. The value on the sailboat was $79,000.
5. CDB Infotek's service (*www.cdb.com*) can locate ownership on vehicles.
6. N.A.D.A. Car and Truck Guides also are a good source of motor vehicle values. And, don't overlook Edmund's web site at *www.edmunds.com/edweb* for market values on new cars.
7. Aircraft ownership searches are available through a private vendor at *www.wdia.com/faa.htm* for a charge.

CALENDARS

Calendars, whether written on an actual calendar, in a calendar notebook, or in the form of a computer database or printout, provide good background information. Often, they serve as links between separate, dissimilar documents by placing them into a chronological pattern.

In Peter's case, his calendar for the date corresponding to the hotel room in Phenix City, Alabama noted "Meeting Carl Tri-State." When Peter was on a business trip to California recently, he blocked out on the calendar the dates June 16-21 with the notation, "Marina-Bev." Calendars can't tell the whole story, but they can reinforce what other records have to say and develop new leads for financial investigation.

LEASES

Following a hunch, Richard ran Marina Del Rey Interests, L.P. on Merlin's California real estate database. He found a property, among several in Southern California, owned by the limited partnership at 1137 Wharf Drive in Marina Del Rey. Among Peter's papers Mary found a lease signed by Peter with the landlord as Marina Del Rey Interests, L.P. for an apartment at 1137 Wharf Drive. The listed tenants were Peter Jackson and Beverly Johnson.

Leases often explain why real property does not appear in a target's name. They also identify hidden relationships.

COLLECTIBLES

Mary did find a rough, handwritten inventory of Peter's coin collection. Consisting mainly of Nineteenth Century American coins, Mary valued the collection, judging from the catalogue purchased through *www.borders.com*, at about $14,000. Cross-checking the collection's list against the actual contents of the safe deposit box, Mary found few discrepancies. In fact, overall, the safe deposit box contained nothing new: the stocks previously discussed, their wills, the deed on their home, and the coin collection.

To determine the value on almost any collectible, numerous

resources exist on the web. *Ebay.com* and *Amazon.com* are just two of the auction sites where the market values of collectibles are easily had. Running a keyword search on almost any web search engine will reveal numerous sites packed with market values on coins, stamps, dolls, antique watches, and so on. In running "coins" on *www.yahoo.com*, Richard uncovered hundreds of sites.

SUMMARY OF INTERNET RESOURCES

Aircraft Registrations-	*www.wdia.com/faa.html* *Also* **CDB Infotek,** *www.cdb.com*
Boats-	**Values:** www.nadaguides.com **Registrations:** *www.state.tx.us* (home page) (The URL for any state just requires the substituting of the two letter code.)
Businesses/Corporations-	**Dun and Bradstreet:** *www.dnb.com* **CDB Infotek:** *www.cdb.com* **Merlin Information Services:** *www.merlindata.com* **OPEN:** *www.openonline.com* **Edgar:** *www.sec.gov/edgarhp.htm* **Experian** (formerly TRW Business Credit): *www.experian.com* **CNN Financial Network:** *www.cnnfn.com* **PR Newswire:** *www.prnewswire.com* **Quicken:** *www.quicken.com/investments/snapshot* **Creditworthy:** *www.creditworthy.com* **Yahoo** (Finance Section): *www.yahoo.com*
Cars, Trucks-	**Values:** *www.edmunds.com/edweb* *www.nadaguides.com* **Registrations:** *www.state.tx.us* *www.cdb.com*
Charitable Organizations-	**National Charities Information**

	Bureau: *www.give.org*
	IRS: *www.irs.ustreas.gov/plain/tax_stats/ soi/ ex_imf.html*
Collectibles-	*www.ebay.com*
	www.amazon.com
	Topic searches with: *www.yahoo.com* **and:** *www.altavista.com*
Database Providers-	**CDB Infotek** (formerly Prentice Hall Online): *www.cdb.com*
	Merlin Information Services: *www.merlindata.com*
	Dialog: *www.dialog.com*
	OPEN: *www.openonline.com*
	KnowX: *www.knowx.com*
	NEXIS/LEXIS (aka Lexis/Nexis): *www.lexis-nexis.com*
	Information America: *www.infoam.com*
Edgar (SEC)-	*www.sec.gov/edgarhp.htm*
Foreign Businesses-	*www.altavista.com*
	www.yahoo.com
	www.snap.com
	www.dnb.com
	www.deja.com
Gale Research-	**InfoTrac:** *www.gale.com/gale/infotrac/icatalog.html*
Insurance Companies-	**A.M. Best:** *www.ambest.com*
Newsgroups-	*www.deja.com*
Newspapers-	**DataTimes:** *www.datatimes.com*
	www.lexis-nexis.com
Real Estate-	**Experian** (formerly TRW Redi): *www.experian.com*
	CDB Infotek
	Merlin Information Services
Securities-	*www.snap.com*
	Edgar
	AOL Interface
	www.yahoo.com
	Prodigy
	Compuserve

SELECTED BIBLIOGRAPHY

Books

Air Service Directory, Inc.: *ABD-Aviation Buyer 's Directory.* Stamford, CT, quarterly.

Association of Certified Fraud Examiners: *Corporate Espionage.* Austin, Texas, 1999.

Beckenham, Kent: *Directory of European Associations,* 3rd ed. Detroit, Gale, 1984.

Benford, Tom: *Welcome to. . . CD-ROM.* New York, MIS Press, 1993.

Bowker, R.R.: *Directory of American Scholars: A Biographical Directory,* 8th ed. New York, Bowker, 1982.

BUC International: *BUC's New Boat Price Guide.* Ft. Lauderdale, FL, annual.

BUC International: *BUC's Used Boat Price Guide.* Ft. Lauderdale, FL, annual.

Bureau of Business Research: *Directory of Texas Manufacturers.* Austin, University of Texas, 1992.

Carroll, John M.: *Confidential Information Sources: Public and Private,* 2nd ed. Stoneham, MA, Butterworth Publications, 1991. A comprehensive book on doing background investigations of individuals. Strongly recommended.

Cole Publications: *Cole's Directory of Austin.* San Antonio, Cole, annual.

Columbia Books: *National Trade and Professional Associations of the United States and Canada and Labor Unions.* Washington, Columbia, 1980.

Cuadra Associates: *Directory of Online databases.* Santa Monica, Cuadra, quarterly.

Council of State Governments The: *State Administrative Officials Classified by Function 1991-1992.* Lexington, KY, 1991. A fine source for determining which state agency regulates a particular industry or profession.

Daniells, Lorna: *Business Information Sources.* Berkeley, CA, University of California Press, 1985.

Darnay, Arsem: *American Salaries and Wages.* Detroit, Gale, 1991.

Dow Jones-Irwin: *The Dow Jones-Irwin Business and Investment Almanac.* Homewood, IL, Dow Jones-Irwin, 1990.

Dun & Bradstreet: *Europe's 10,000 Largest Companies.* New York, 1982.

Dun & Bradstreet: *Selected Key Business Ratios in 125 Lines of Business.* New York, 1981.

Dun's Marketing Services: *Million Dollar Directory.* Parsippany, annual.

Europa: *The Europa Year Book.* London, Europa, annual.

Fuld, Leonard: *Competitor Intelligence.* New York, John Wiley, 1985. Excellent overview of business intelligence techniques. Money reference sources listed. Strong on foreign business and financial sources.

Gale Research: *Biography and Genealogy Master Index.* Detroit, Gale, 1980.

Gale Research: *Directories in Print.* Detroit, Gale, 1990.

Gale Research: *Directory of Special Libraries and Information Centers.* Detroit, Gale, 1990.

Gale Research: *Encyclopedia of Associations.* Detroit, Gale, 1993.

Gale Research: *Encyclopedia of Associations, International.* Detroit, Gale, 1993.

Gale Research: *Newsletters in Print.* Detroit, Gale, 1993.

Gale Research: *Research Centers Directory.* Detroit, Gale, 1993.

Gale Research: *Ward 's Business Directory of U.S. Private and Public Companies.* Detroit, Gale, 1989.

Hoy, Michael: *Directory of U.S. Mail Drops.* Port Townsend, Loompanics Unlimited, 1987.

H.W. Wilson Co.: *Biography Index.* New York, biennial.

Insured Aircraft Title Service, Inc.: *United States Civil Aircraft Registry.* Oklahoma City, monthly.

Internal Revenue Service: *Cumulative List of Organizations.* Washington, IRS, bimonthly.

Internal Revenue Service: *IRS Special Agent's Guide to the Money Laundering Control Act of 1986.* Washington, IRS, 1987.

Kahaner, Larry: *Competitive Intelligence.* New York, Simon and Schuster, 1996.

Katz, Bill, & Katz, Linda S.: *Magazines for Libraries,* 7th ed. New York, R.R. Bowker, 1992.

King, Dennis: *Get the Facts on Anyone.* New York, Prentice-Hall, 1992. The comprehensive introductory text on public records research. Well written and insightful. Covers a number of financial scams. A must book for financial investigators!

Lavin, Michael R.: *Business Information: How to Find It, How to Use It.* Phoenix, Oryx Press, 1987.

Lesko, Matthew: *Lesko's Info-Power.* Kensington, MD, Information, USA, 1990.

Lesko, Matthew: *Information, U.S.A.* New York, Penguin Books, 1986.

Levine, John R., & Young, Margaret Levine: *The Internet for Dummies Quick Reference.* Foster City, CA., IDG Books, 1994.

Marquis Who's Who: *Directory of Medical Specialists.* Chicago, biennial.

Marquis Who's Who: *Marquis Who's Who Index to Who's Who Books.* Chicago, 1985.

Martindale-Hubbell: *Martindale-Hubbell Law Directory.* Summit, NJ, annual.

McCormick, Mona: *The New York Times Guide to Reference Materials,* rev. ed. New York, Signet, 1986.

McCormick, Mona: *The Fiction Writer's Research Handbook.* New York, Plume, 1988.

Meckler Publishing: *CD-ROMs in Print.* Westport, CT, 1992.

Mendell, Ronald L.: *How to Conduct Business Investigations and Competitive Intelligence Gathering.* Austin, TX, Thomas Investigative Publications, 1997.

Mendell, Ronald L.: *Investigating Computer Crime: A Primer for Security Managers.* Springfield, IL, Charles C Thomas, 1998.

National Automotive Dealers Association: *N.A.D.A. Official Used Car Guide.* McLean, monthly.

National Institute on Economic Crime: Kramer, W. Michael: *Investigative Techniques in Complex Financial Crimes,* 3rd. ed. Washington, 1990.

Oxbridge Publishing: *Standard Periodical Directory.* New York, Oxbridge, 1964-irregular.

Pankau, Edmund J.: *Checking It Out! Everyone's Guide to investigation.* Houston Cloak & Data Press, 1990. A basic introduction to investigation. Has some useful social psychology about swindlers. Good sections on public records.

Rand McNally: *Rand McNally International Bankers Directory.* Chicago, 1986.

Rugge, Sue and Glossbrenner, Alfred: *The Information Broker's Handbook.* Blue Ridge Summit, PA, McGraw-Hill, 1992.

Scott, Robert: *The Investigator's Little Black Book 2.* Beverly Hills, CA, Crime Time Publishing Co., 1998. An encyclopedia of investigative sources.

Securities and Exchange Commission: *Directory of Companies Required to File Annual Reports with the SEC.* Washington, SEC, 1993.

Slocum, Robert B.: *Biographical Dictionaries and Related Works,* 2nd ed. Detroit, Gale, 1986.

Texas State Bar: *Checklists (Family Law).* Austin, TX, 1998.

Texas State Bar: *The Texas Legal Directory.* Dallas, Legal Directories Publishing, 1993.

Thomas Publishing: *Thomas Register of American Manufacturers.* New York, annual. The encyclopedia of who makes what. Organized by company name and by product.

Thorndike, David: *Thorndike Encyclopedia of Banking and Financial Tables.* Boston, Warren, Gorham and Lamont, 1987.

Ullmann, John; Honeyman, Steve, Editors: *The Reporter's Handbook.* New York, St. Martin's Press, 1983. A comprehensive guide to public records. Excellent chapters on business investigations and bankruptcies.

U.S. Dept. of Commerce-Bureau of the Census: *Statistical Abstract of the United States.* Washington, 1992.

U.S. Dept. of Commerce: *United States Industrial Outlook.* Washington, annual.

U.S. Dept. of Labor: *Austin Area Wage Survey.* Washington, Labor, 1987.

Washington Researchers Publishing: *How to Find Information About Companies.* Washington, 1988.

Wasserman, Paul; O'Brien, Jacqueline, ed.: *Statistics Sources,* 13th ed. Detroit, Gale, 1990.

Woy, James, ed.: *Encyclopedia of Business Information Sources.* Detroit, Gale, 1990.

Wurman, Richard Saul: *Information Anxiety.* New York, Doubleday, 1989. A road map through the information age. Wurman argues that the best way to deal with the information onslaught is to first understand its organization. Once you know how to pigeonhole information, you can use it to your advantage.

Yacht Owners Register, Inc.: *Register of American Yachts.* Boston, 1991.

Articles

Cervantes, George A.: General Financial Investigations. *The Legal Investigator,* 21:1, 1991.

Francis, Joan A.: Bankruptcy—A Vault of Information. *The Legal Investigator,* 21:1, 1991.

Hart, Alan: Financial Cases' Investigation Techniques. *The Legal Investigator,* 19:2, 1989.

Mendell, Ronald L.: Business Intelligence Techniques and the Legal Investigator. *The Legal Investigator,* 15:3, 1986.

Mendell, Ronald L.: Medical Malpractice: New Considerations. *The Legal Investigator,* 21:4, 1992.

Mendell, Ronald L.: E-mail for Investigators. *The Legal Investigator,* 22:4, 1993.

Mendell, Ronald L.: How Investigators Can Use CD-ROMs. *The Legal Investigator,* 23:2, 1993.

Mendell, Ronald L.: Is the Internet Just a Web of Misinformation? *Security Management,* 43:6, June 1996.

Pankau, Edmund: Discovering Hidden Assets. *The Legal Investigator,* 21:1, 1991.

Schatzman, John R.: Investigating Real Estate and Mortgage Fraud. *The Legal Investigator,* 22:1, 1992.

INDEX

A

Abstract of judgment, 21
Address histories, 10, 79
Agency law, 70
Aircraft records, 30, 37-38, 177
Alcoholic beverage licenses, 22
America Online (AOL), 52
American Society for Industrial Security (ASIS), 48
Associations (*see* Sources of information)
Attorney General, state charitable fraud division, 103

B

Background investigations (*see* Individuals, background investigations *and* Security manager tools)
Balance sheets, vii, 96-97
Bank Secrets Act, 83
Banking information
    general, 161
    Rand McNally International Banker Directory, 100
    statements and checks, 11, 166, 176
    teller's work, 83
Bankruptcy records, 18, 30, 31, 33-34, 82, 155
Basic business reference sources (*see* Business sources)
Basic identifiers (*see* Identifiers, basic)
Better Business Bureau, 53, 97, 103
Biographical sources
    Biography and Genealogy Master Index, 17, 57, 163, 181
    Biography Index, 57, 182
    research centers, 57
Boats, 36-37, 64, 177
Bogus assets and liabilities, 74, 76
Building code department, 118, 124
Businesses (*see also* Business sources *and* Corporations)

background, 132-134
balance sheets, 96-99
cash flow of, 96
credit reports, 103, 104
fly-by-night, 53
foreign, 86-89, 173-174
hidden interest in, 75
history of, 97
interlocking companies, 156-157
key business ratios (*see* Key business ratios)
locating, 98
nonprofit, 103
unincorporated, 102
Business intelligence, 54, 115-117, 130-135
Business sources
    advanced
        business intelligence (*see* Business intelligence)
        experts (*see* Experts)
        interviews (*see* Techniques, interviewing)
        ratios (*see* Key business ratios)
    basic
        aircraft, 105
        boats, 105
        CD-ROMs, 99
        corporate veil, piercing the, 106-108
        credit reports, 103
        form, 110-112
        personal property, 105
        real estate, 99
        reference works, 100
        SEC reports, 104
        state filings, 100-102
        vehicles, 105
Business sources
    CD-ROM, books on, 54-55
    foreign, 55
    general, 53-56
    newspapers, 54
    print (*see also* Directories)
        Encyclopedia of Business Information

185

Sources, 54
How to Find Information About Companies, 100

C

Calendars, 167, 178
CD-ROMs, vii, 5, 6, 12, 13, 16, 21, 30, 32, 35, 51, 54, 77, 87-88, 153, 169
  legal, 30, 51
  newspapers, 21, 32, 35, 87-88, 153
  Yellow Pages, 13
Charitable organizations, 103
Civil court records, 14-15, 22, 29, 30
Collectibles (*see also* Hidden assets), 85-86, 178-179
Competitive Intelligence, 134, 182
Competitor Intelligence, 87, 117, 126, 129, 181
Comprehensive Dissertation Index, 126
Computer databases
  ABI/INFORM, 24, 29, 31, 32, 51
  Business Periodical Index, 6, 32, 51
  CDB Infotek (*formerly* Prentice-Hall Online), 23, 29, 32, 42, 47, 48, 54, 77, 152, 162
  cross-checking of, 4
  DIALOG, 6, 24, 29, 47, 51, 52, 54, 87, 162
  Disclosure/Spectrum, 24
  Dun and Bradstreet, 42, 53, 54, 55, 58
  InfoTrac, 22, 29, 30, 51
  legal
    Legal Resource Index, 6, 30, 32, 51, 161-162
    WESTLAW, 30, 31, 32, 162
  mailing lists, 24, 29
  Merlin Information Services, 42, 48, 77, 169
  newspapers
    DataTimes, 22, 30, 32, 54, 98
    National Newspaper Index, 6, 22, 51
    NEXIS/LEXIS, 5, 6, 22, 29, 30, 31, 32, 50-51, 98, 157
  municipal, 8, 16
  police, 16
Corporations
  alter ego of, ix, 106-109
  dead and dissolved (*see* Hidden assets)
  incorporation file, 95
  officer/director searches, 21, 30, 40, 51, 168-170

  piercing the veil of, ix, 106-109
  searches, 168-170
  shell, 34
Court records, civil (*see also* Lawsuits), 14-15, 22, 29, 30
Credit cards, 174
Credit header, 23, 29, 49
Credit services
  businesses, 55, 158-160
  credit header, 29, 49
  credit history, 80
  Dun and Bradstreet, 55, 158, 169
  Experian, 6, 55, 58, 158
Criminal records, 22, 29, 30, 77, 78
Customers, 96

D

Data (*see also* Business intelligence)
  analyzing, 142-145
  association summary, 143
  banking summary, 143-145
  correlation of, viii, 3, 7, 118, 131-132, 139-142, 151
  organizing, 13, 19, 139-142, 154
  reliability of, 130-131
  validity of, 131-132
Death certificates, 18
Directories (*see also* Business sources, print)
  Business Information: How to Find It, How to Use It, 100, 182
  city, 20
  crisscross, 15, 29, 60, 63
  Directories in Print, 17, 54, 55, 125, 126, 181
  Directory of Texas Manufacturers, 53, 181
  Directory of Special Libraries and Information Centers, 88, 181
  foreign, 87
  Million Dollar Directory, 53, 54, 87, 181
  old, 17
  professional, 17
  Thomas Register of Manufacturers, 53, 54, 125, 183
  United States Industrial Outlook, 100, 183
Divorce investigations, ix, 31, 165-180
Drive-by of residence, 26, 59-64, 65-68
Driver's licenses, 15, 21, 30
Dun's Business Identification Service, 53, 98
DVD, 6, 12

E

Edgar (SEC), 170
E-Mail, 52
Experts
  accountants, 84, 86, 90
  bank loan officers, 71
  overseas or offshore specialists, 88
  security dealers, 74
  sources for, 125-127

F

Fair Credit Reporting Act (FCRA), 3, 23, 50
Financial investigations, security managers, a
  tool for, 76-78
Financial statements, 16-17, 72, 73-74, 79, 166,
  173-174
FIND/SVP, 133
Foreign accounts and businesses (*see* Hidden
  assets)
Forms
  association summary, 144
  banking summary, 145
  business asset summary, basic, 110-112
  business credit, 104
  business profile, 101
  hidden assets, 93-94
  individual summary, 44-46
  interview contact, 136-137
  pedigree, 28-29
  personal property, 109
  plant visit, 122-124
  residence check, 65-68
  universal public record, 148-150
Fundamental accounting equation, 96-97

G

General partners, masquerading as limited
  partners, 84
Get the Facts on Anyone, 55, 182

H

Hidden assets
  accountant
    forensic, 84, 90
    target's, 86
  annuities, 82

businesses, list of, 80
cashier checks, 83
checklist form, 93-94
collectibles, 85-86
common hiding places, 80-81
credit card statements, 80
dead and dissolved corporations, 84-85
discovery techniques, 79-80
financial dodges
  overpayments to IRS, 89-90
  sweetheart lawsuits, 32, 34, 90-91
income tax records, 80
life insurance, 81-82, 166
limited partnerships, 74, 83-84
money orders, 82-83
mortgage paydown, 81
names, in other, 89
negotiable instruments, 82-83
overseas or offshore accounts, 86-89, 173-
  174
safe deposit boxes, 85-86, 167-168, 178-179
savings bonds, 83
stockbroker accounts, 85
telephone bills, 80
travel documents, 80
traveler's checks, 83
unreported income, 74-76
Hiding places (*see* Hidden assets)
Historical records, 17, 23, 29, 143
Human sources
  businesses, local, 26
  collection agencies, 26
  creditors, 26
  delivery persons, 26
  enemies, 32, 125
  general, vii, 125-128
  landlords, 26
  neighbors, 26, 63
  professional or trade organizations, 26-27
  public service organizations, 26
  relatives and associates, in locating, 26-27
  social groups, 27
  stockbrokers, 85
  suppliers (*see* Suppliers)

I

Identifiers, basic
  common sources of, 10-12
  date of birth (DOB), 8-9, 14, 16, 17, 18

general, viii, 8-19
importance of, 8-9
lesser known sources of, 15-16
other common sources, 15
SSN (*see* Social security number)
summary, 18-19
Income
disclosed earnings, 73
estimating, 71, 75-76
income tax returns, 175
unreported, 74-76
wages, 70-71
Individuals
advanced sources for
accident cases, 70
basic sources, difference from, 69-70
financial statements, 72, 73-74
governmental sources, 71-72
lawsuits, 76
real estate records, 73
unreported income, 74-76
wage earnings, 70-71
background investigations, ix, 49, 76-78
basic sources for
aircraft, 37-38, 177
bankruptcy records, 33-34
boats, 36-37, 177
criminal (*see* Criminal records)
occupation, 35
officer/director searches, 40, 168-170
real estate records, 30, 40-42, 176-177
summary form, 44-46
vehicles, 21, 177
credit reports (*see* Credit header *and* Credit services)
pedigree, 28-29
Information Anxiety, 13
Information brokers, 3, 6, 47-50
Information Broker's Handbook, 48
Internal Revenue Service (IRS)
Cumulative List of Organizations, 55, 103, 182
Form 990, 55-56, 103
limited partnerships, and, 83-84
money laundering, 88
overpayments to (*see* Hidden assets)
web sites, 170
International sources (*see also* Hidden assets)
directories, 55

general, 86-89
Internet (*see also* Web sites)
aircraft, 177
bank statements, 176
boats, 177
calendars, 178
charities, 170
checklists, 165-166, 178-180
collectibles, 178-179
corporations and businesses, 168-170
credit cards, 174
Edgar (SEC), 170
financial statements, 173-174
general, ix, 4
income tax returns, 175
insurance companies, 166, 171-172
IRS, 170
leases, 178
motor vehicles, 177
newsgroups, ix, 29, 56-57, 173
newspapers, 133
real estate, 176
search engines, 29
securities, 170-171
Interrogatories, 14, 82
Investigating Computer Crime: A Primer for Security Managers, 78, 182
Investigator's Little Black Book 2, 168, 170, 183
IRSC (information broker), 48, 49

J

Justice of the Peace courts, 16

K

Key business ratios, 95, 129-130, 162-163

L

Lawsuits, 14-15, 30, 69
Legal Investigator, 48, 183-184
Libraries
OCLC, 22
public, 21, 52, 97
university, 22, 30, 86, 97
Life insurance (*see* Hidden assets)
Limited partnerships (*see* Hidden assets)

M

Manuals, state and federal, 18
Martindale-Hubbell Law Directory, 17, 182
Military discharges, 22
Money orders (see Hidden assets)
Motor vehicle records, 21, 30, 36, 155, 177
   "alpha" search, 36
Municipal court databases, 8, 16, 141

N

N.A.D.A. guides (motor vehicles), 71, 75
Names, 9-10
Newsgroups (*see* Internet, newsgroups)
Newspapers (*see also* Computer databases), 5,
   6, 22, 29, 30, 31, 32, 50-51, 54, 157-158
National Association of Legal Investigators
   (NALI), 48
Non-financial documents, vii, 3, 22, 29, 30,
   77, 78

O

Occupational information, sources of, 35
Online Computer Library Center (OCLC),
   22, 31, 88
Organizing information
   data (*see* Data)
   tools for, 12-14
OSHA, 119, 120, 124
Overseas and offshore accounts (*see* Hidden
   assets)

P

Patents, 51, 151
Pedigree form, 28-29
Personal bonds, criminal, 14, 154
Place of birth (POB), 11
Planning commission, 114, 118, 124
Plant visits, 113-124
Prentice-Hall Online (*see* Computer databas-
   es, CDB Infotek)
Privacy issues, 3
Probate court records, 30
Professional directories, 17
Public records (*see* Sources of information,
   public records)

R

Real estate records
   basic source, as a, 30
   grantor/grantee, 40
   other jurisdictions, locating in, 41-42, 176
   searches, 40-42, 155-156, 167
   tax appraisal district, 63, 118, 155-156
Records, governmental, 18, 38-40, 71-72
Relatives and associates, identifying
   basic sources for, 20-22
   checklist, 29
   human sources, with, 26-27, 29
   local newspaper on CD-ROM, using, 21
   motor vehicle address searches, using, 21
   other miscellaneous sources for, 22
   other states and localities, in, 22-26
Reports to client
   businesses, on, 147-148
   individuals, on, 145-146
Requests for production, 14
Research sources (table), 58
Royalties, 22

S

Safe deposit box, 86, 167-168, 178
Securities, 170-171
Securities and Exchange Commission (SEC),
   24, 51, 54, 95
Security managers, 76-78
Security manager tools, ix, 76-78
Security Management, 48
Sherlock Holmes, 20, 61
Smoke screens, vii
Social security number (SSN)
   identifier, as a basic, 9, 14, 17, 18
   information brokers, and, 49
   relatives and associates, for locating, 24-
      26, 29
   table, 25
Sources of information
   associations, 55, 126
   banking (*see* Banking information)
   biographical (*see* Biographical sources)
   businesses (*see* Businesses *and* Business
      sources)
   databases (*see* Computer databases *and*
      Internet)

directories (*see* Directories)
discovery (*see* Techniques)
experts (*see* Experts)
foreign accounts and businesses (*see* Hidden assets)
history (*see* Historical centers)
human (*see* Human sources)
income (*see* Income)
individuals (*see* Individuals)
information brokers (*see* Information brokers)
Inside information (*see* Human sources)
Internet (*see* Internet)
land use (*see* Building code department; Planning commission; Zoning commission)
lawsuits (*see* Lawsuits *and* Court records)
libraries (*see* Libraries)
newspapers (*see* Computer databases *and* Newspapers)
non-financial documents (*see* Non-financial documents)
occupational (*see* Occupational information)
public records, vii, ix, 14-15, 22, 29, 30, 42, 43
public records shortcuts, 42
real estate (*see* Real estate)
suppliers (*see* Suppliers)
Special interest groups (SIGs), 52
Standard Industrial Classification Code (SIC), 126
Statistical Abstract of the United States, 75
Stonewall, vii
Suppliers, 95, 96, 125
Surveillance, vii, 61, 125-126, 131
Sweetheart lawsuits (*see* Hidden assets)

T

Tax appraisal district, 42, 59, 63, 118, 155-156
Tax liens, 22, 30, 35, 39
Techniques
accountants, using, 84, 90
buildings, analysis of, 118-120
business intelligence (*see* Business intelligence)
checks, using, 82-83
cross-checking, 32
discovery, 79-80
estimating income, 74-76
interviewing, 91, 127-128, 136-137
life insurance transactions, 81-82
link diagrams, 144, 164
NASD securities dealer, using a, 74
personnel, for reviewing, 76-78
photographs, using, 113
piercing the corporate veil, 106-109
pretext calls, 84, 96, 127
"reading an office," 115-116
real estate, locating, 40-42
real estate records, analyzing, 73
record searching, 11-12
scanning for information, 5
timelines and chronologies, 23, 142-143, 164
unreported income, calculating, 74-76
Telephone book, 13-14, 18, 23
Termination of investigations, 69-70
Texas Association of Licensed Investigators (TALI), 48
Trash
identifiers, as a source of basic, 11
reading the, 61-63
value of, 61-62

U

UCC filings, 6, 22, 23, 30, 35, 39-43, 77, 81, 84, 152, 153, 154
Uniform Commercial Code (*see* UCC filings, *see also* Sources of information, public records)

V

Voters' registration, 11, 22, 29, 35, 156

W

Web sites
business news, 170
general list of, 179-180
information brokers, 48
search engines, 169
Who's Who, 17, 57

Y

Yellow Pages, 29

Z

Zoning commission, 114, 119, 124